THE BEER CAN BY THE HIGHWAY

Other books by the author

HALF A TRUTH IS BETTER THAN NONE: SOME
  UNSYSTEMATIC CONJECTURES ABOUT ART,
  DISORDER, AND AMERICAN EXPERIENCE
PARTNERS IN BANKING: AN HISTORICAL PORTRAIT
  OF A GREAT PRIVATE BANK
THE COLUMBIA HISTORICAL PORTRAIT OF NEW YORK:
  AN ESSAY IN GRAPHIC HISTORY
MADE IN AMERICA: THE ARTS IN MODERN
  CIVILIZATION
ADVENTURES OF AMERICA, 1857–1900

Edited volumes

THE NEW YORK GUIDEBOOK
WHEN WOMEN LOOK AT MEN, *with Janice Farrar Thadeus*

JOHN A. KOUWENHOVEN

The Beer Can by the Highway

Essays on What's "American"
about America

Foreword by Ralph Ellison

THE JOHNS HOPKINS UNIVERSITY PRESS
BALTIMORE AND LONDON

Originally published 1961 by Doubleday & Company

The Johns Hopkins University Press
701 West 40th Street
Baltimore, Maryland 21211
The Johns Hopkins Press Ltd., London

The paper used in this publication meets the minimum
requirements of American National Standard for
Information Sciences—Permanence of Paper for Printed
Library Materials, ANSI Z39.48-1984.

Library of Congress Cataloging-in-Publication Data

Kouwenhoven, John Atlee, 1909–
    The beer can by the highway.

    Reprint. Originally published: Garden City, N.Y.:
Doubleday, 1961.
    Includes index.
    1. United States—Civilization—1945–
I. Title.
E169.1.K67   1988   973.92   87-46303
ISBN 0-8018-3667-0
ISBN 0-8018-3653-0 (pbk.)

CONTENTS

FOREWORD

THERE SITS ON A GLASS-TOPPED, stainless steel table in our living room a small goblet with slitted sides that swirl upward from its round, pinched shaft to form a bowl that's "bellied"—to borrow a figure from T. S. Eliot—"like the fig's fruit." This surprising object was created on a busy downtown New York street by an Afro-American craftsman-vendor out of a Shasta Lemon Lime Soda can. My wife, who had watched its magical creation (during which the craftsman knelt on the sidewalk carrying on an open-ended, P. T. Barnum spiel), was so delighted that she bought it right out of his flickering fingers. And when she arrived home all excited and began explaining the origin of her prize I took a look, felt a light bulb glow up in my head, and exclaimed, "Well now, John Kouwenhoven, it's not exactly a *beer* can, but it's more than ample proof that somebody out there is continuing to affirm your insights into the interaction between the cultivated and vernacular modes as they find expression in American culture!"

And of course they are, whether it be our street craftsman, the artists of Pop Art, architects responsible for the rash of skyscrapers that are darkening

the streets of New York, the exponents of the latest
variant of rock-and-roll, or the designers of automobiles who have found a more functional form for
hoods, tops, and fenders. And for all the reasons—
geographical, political, economic, technological, and
aesthetic—that Kouwenhoven analyzes in *The Beer
Can by the Highway.*

But for the moment let's keep an eye on our
gobletized soda can and consider what must have
happened before this marvelous product of vernacular prestidigitation became possible: A beverage can
worth all of five cents (if returned to a supermarket)
was emptied of its bubbly contents and discarded—
it doesn't matter whether beside a highway or in the
aisle of a subway car, the point here is that in the
course of its transformation this sibling to a beer can
escaped its expected, routine fate of recycling as
scrap metal and became, instead, an *objet trouvé.*
And then, as though to challenge our easy definitions
of "waste" and "raw material," *high* style and *low,*
and rush us back to Kouwenhoven's writings, our
can lands in the hands of a "vernacular" craftsman
who proceeds (and without attempting to erase any
evidence of its past identity as mere container—
neither paint, gleam, computerized bar-code, nor
lettering) to transform it into a charming classical
form.

Here we have a poker-faced American joke in
which an object democratically available to even the
commonest of common citizens ends up mocking

both the elaborate technology and economic motive which gave it birth, while flaunting the impulses, vernacular and classical, that interacted in a complex process of antagonistic cooperation to give it its present shape and setting. For in its metamorphosis toward its present form our can had progressed, thanks to industrial technology, from a handful of common ore to a mass-produced utilitarian vessel, and then it had been transformed by an anonymous craftsman of pluralistic American background and taste into a work of art.

"But wait, hold!" you say. "A can is a can is a can, and as such a form admirably fitted to an admirable function. But that gaudy, split-sided thing you're describing couldn't contain a bubble of ale or bail the spray from a boat!" Which, if you insist upon looking only for the *old* in the new, is quite true. But while it is evident that our gobletized can is no longer functional as in its old, utilitarian state, it has assumed nevertheless a *new*, and most useful, function indeed. For now, as it sits on its Miesian table, not only does it delight its viewers' eyes, but it challenges us to think with playful seriousness about the relationship between America's democratic ideals and its culture. Yes, and about the ways in which those ideals inspirit not only our diverse citizenry but even the humblest of products and processes, sports and games, nightmares and dreams. And it challenges us to think about such matters as carefully as Kouwenhoven has thought about the

Americanness of everything that binds us. From our technology-propelled search for national self-consciousness as it is affected by our pervasive self-doubt, to our volatile mixture of vernacular and cultivated taste, to the designs of our skyscrapers, the nature of jazz, comic strips, and advertising, to our grids of beer-can-strewn streets and highways.

The Beer Can by the Highway was first published in 1961, and since that time it has been quietly teaching Americans to discern in things both great and small, dignified and pedestrian, that which is essentially "American" about American civilization. It is a work that springs from deep within that rich segment of the American grain which gave us the likes of Emerson and Whitman, Horatio Greenough and Constance Rourke—yes, and Mark Twain—and was written by a critic who has looked long and hard at American culture with that native mixture of comic and tragic vision which is so necessary if we are to make sense of our diverse, pluralistic society. Fortunately, Kouwenhoven is a writer who possesses the irreverent eloquence to make us recognize the old in the new and the new that is emergent in old processes and objects, attitudes, and customs.

Which is to say that he has an insightful knowledge of history, taste, and design. Thus he is able to make us see the negative in our vaunted positives, and the positives in our down-played negatives. Best of all, during a period when we are once again evaluating the meaning of the Constitution and assessing the gains and losses of the past two hundred years, he makes us aware of the intricate ways in which our ways of life mesh and/or clash with our democratic ideals. A mixture of scholarly erudition and wry, vernacular perception, *The Beer Can by the Highway* arrives at its larger insights through a careful scrutiny of small facts and processes, thereby making its perceptions democratically available to all readers, whether learned or casual. Since I have long rated it as one of the most provocatively American of books, I am not surprised, only delighted, that during these times of crisis, of abundance and famine, of controversy over who shall interpret the Constitution, of stock market dives, startling new technologies, atomic piles and industrial waste, and garbage barges making futile trips through international seas in search of a noncontroversial burial site, the voluble *Beer Can* has taken on, like its Shasta cousin, a new and most vibrant life.

RALPH ELLISON

November 1987

THOSE WHO READ THESE ESSAYS in the order in which they are presented will find, I trust, that they build upon one another. They may be read in random order, but I hope they will not be, for I have done my best to write (and rewrite) them in a way which makes each of the later ones evolve from those which precede it.

The first one tries, by indirection, to suggest the limitations of the point of view from which I have looked at the United States. The next two introduce the general question of what is "American" in our civilization and suggest some answers.

The fourth and fifth essays touch upon some of the ways in which education and our ideas of "culture" may unfit us for the "American" world. Then come four essays dealing with the ways in which "American" qualities are expressed (or stifled) in the arts of design, with particular emphasis on architecture, industrial design, and advertising layout.

The final essay, which gathers up threads of idea and attitude from the earlier essays, will, I hope, lead the reader as it did the writer to look with unaccustomed eyes at some contemporary manifestations of the energies which are likely to shape our future.

J.A.K.

December 20, 1960

Preliminary Glance
at an American Landscape

FROM THE BLISTER-DOME of the Wabash Railway's *Blue Bird,* en route from St. Louis to Chicago, the spring landscape of central Illinois is one of wide, level horizons with now and then a clump of leafed-out willows or a brief row of maples or elms which have budded enough to look hazy. It is a land of pale coffee-colored fields, darkened in irregular blotches where cloud shadows lie and in strips where a tractor-drawn disc harrow has recently passed. A lone man driving a tractor is the only human being you are likely to see for miles, but there are many other living things: cattle—black, or black and white, and still winter-fuzzy—standing or lying in the unplowed fields; pigs and sheep whose young scamper away from the fenced railroad track when the train passes, though their elders are accustomed and remain still; and quite often a pheasant, green neck feathers shining in the sun, standing close to the track, always with his back turned to the passing train, looking over his shoulder at it but not otherwise disturbed.

The only city you go through is Decatur, a momentary collection of factories, warehouses, and handsome grain elevators, and a business district with some stone buildings of modest dimensions. Most of the towns you go through are small and irregularly square, with streets at right angles to the railroad, many of which do not cross the track but stop short at earth mounds partly covered with grass. Each town has a corrugated sheet-metal grain elevator and a Quonset warehouse or two near the wooden station. The houses are wood, with fruit trees blooming in their board-fenced yards. But there are almost no people in sight, just a few cars moving in the streets or parked at the curbs. And in less than a minute you are out on the prairie again.

Occasionally the level fields are studded with shining ponds, and now and then you see small streams whose flashing surfaces are almost flush with the fields they flow through, or shallow gullies banked with tin cans and bottles which glitter in the sun. Running alongside the track all the way, three tiers of shining wires dip from and rise to the crossbars on the telegraph poles—each of the three crossbars with room for ten bright insulators, some missing, leaving gaps like broken rake teeth. Sometimes the ground bordering the track also dips and rises where the right of way has been sliced down to grade through long, flowing swells of land. But the only real break in the general flatness is a huge eroded mesa, man-made from the waste of what may be strip-mining operations, which stretches along

west of the track for miles, somewhere near Red-
dick or Essex judging by the timetable.

Most of the time there is just the wide, flat
landscape of harrow-smoothed earth, ruled into
squares by lines of wire fence strung on thin metal
posts (not split wooden posts, as in New England),
and along the fences there is a fringe of the dry,
blond husks of last year's uncut grass, with now and
then a large, unaccountable sheet of wilted brown
paper caught on the wire barbs. Once in a huge,
immaculate field near Symerton, roughly forty-seven
miles out of Chicago, I saw a rock. It was about
the size and shape of a dented watermelon, but no
one had bothered to move it; the parallel harrow
tracks in the smooth dirt diverged to avoid it, then
came together again.

Once in a while you see white roads taped
across the landscape, and if they cross the track the
diesel honks at them. Once in a while you see a
lonely schoolhouse, usually of wood, with a flag
flying briskly from a pole in front and a yellow bus
standing in the grassless yard. Once in a while a
field is dotted with round metal grain bins with
cone-shaped roofs, looking like a battery of stumpy,
unlaunchable rockets. And once in a while, too, near
one of the clumps of trees, you see a white farm-
house, with red or white barns—big barns, with venti-
lators on their roofs looking like little barns strad-
dling the ridgepoles of the big ones. Near the houses
tall windmills stand on spindly iron legs, mostly with

broken blades in their fans, and almost every farm has a gawky television antenna in the yard as tall as, or taller than, the windmill.

This is a landscape which a century ago looked to a Chicago newspaperman like "the untilled and almost untrodden pastures of God." Standing with a group of excursionists in the middle of the rolling prairies, the reporter, Benjamin F. Taylor, felt as if he were in the center of a tremendous dish.

> Not a tree nor a living thing in sight; not a sign that man had ever been an occupant of the planet . . . The great blue sky was set down exactly upon the edge of the dish, like the cover of a tureen, and there we were, pitifully belittled.

A century later the pastures of God are well-tilled and much trodden. The prairie has become, in fact, a technological landscape: subdivided by wire fences, smoothed by tractors, tied to the urban-industrial world by wires, roads, and rails, and by the invisible pulses felt in the lofty antennas. The height of those antennas measures the strength of the city's pull. As you leave St. Louis they grow taller and taller until, in central Illinois they outtop and almost outnumber the trees. As you approach Chicago they grow shorter until, when you reach the suburban landscape of supermarkets, drive-ins, and rows of little square houses with little square lawns, they need be only small, solicitous bundles of branching wire rods attached to the house chimneys.

The prairie landscape no longer belittles man. It is still vast, and you see very few people as you watch from a train window. But man's technology has modified everything from the texture of the earth itself to the stance of the pheasants.

This landscape, through which I last traveled three years ago, came freshly to my mind as I began to assemble and revise the essays in this book. It did so, I think, because it embodies a number of the forms and patterns which seem to me to be characteristic of a civilization based as ours is upon a distinctive blend of technology and a somewhat untidy but dynamic form of democracy. And it is with some of these characteristic forms and patterns, and the indigenous energies they express, that these essays are primarily concerned.

There are other American landscapes, some of which embody forms and patterns that seem to have little in common with those of the prairies: the landscape of Maryland's trim and cultivated Eastern Shore; the barbaric splendor of the Southwest's mesas and canyons; the grim and powerful landscape of River Rouge; and—more like the prairies than at first appears—the New York skyline.

The most endearing and comfortable landscape, to me, is in Vermont, where I spend the summers on a farm which lies like a large green saddle blanket on the small of the back of a mountainous ridge along the western border of the state. Eastward from the farm you can look down into the domesticated Vermont valleys of Pawlet and Dorset, with pasture clearings running well up the enclosing slopes. Westward you look out over a widening, open-ended valley where the tree-hidden village of Rupert lies, where dogs bark distantly in the evening, and where an occasional light blinks through the trees after dark. At the far, open end of the valley the D & H Railroad comes down from the north and curves westward into New York State toward the Hudson and the Susquehanna. You cannot see the trains but when the wind is right—when rain is coming—you can hear the imitation steam-whistle which the railroad, in tune with the new industrial sentimentality, has substituted for barking horns on its diesels. And beyond the valley's open end the continent rolls gently westward through the Mohawk Valley and then invisibly onward past the Great Lakes, lifting easily across the prairies and plains. You can believe that if the atmosphere were glass-clear and the earth did not curve you could see two thirds of the way to the Pacific, for there is nothing high enough to block the view till you come to the Laramie Range and the Big Horns. Closed and friendly to the east, open and inviting to the west, it is a likable landscape.

It is, I suppose, the landscape of this eastward-and-westward-looking Vermont farm, superimposed upon the landscape of New York's skyline, which controls the point of view from which I have looked at America. But the characteristic landscape of the America I have looked at in these essays seems to me to be the "interminable and stately prairies," as Walt Whitman called them, ruled off by roads and fences into a mathematical grid. They have become, as Whitman thought they would become, the home of "America's distinctive ideas and distinctive realities." They produced Abraham Lincoln and the city of Chicago—both of which are ideas as well as realities and both of which seem to me, at least, to be distinctively American.

The Dispraising
of America*

SOME UN-AMERICAN ADVICE

TO NON-AMERICANS

* This essay grew out of a talk to a group of foreign students who had come to the United States on Fulbright scholarships. The group, which included citizens of several African and Asian nations as well as some Europeans, were gathered at the Institute of International Education, on invitation of the Mills College Club of New York, March 10, 1959.

I IMAGINE THAT one of the most curious, one of the oddest, things that non-Americans notice in America is what might be called the American's self-consciousness about his American-ness. We have been like that for many years—from the very beginning, in fact.

The first published answer to the question "What is an American?" appeared in 1782—just one year after the battle of Yorktown victoriously ended six years of fighting for American independence. The question forms the title of a much-quoted chapter in *Letters from an American Farmer; Describing Certain Provincial Situations, Manners, and Customs, Not Generally Known.*

This book, which first posed the self-conscious "American" question, was written in the English language, for an English audience, by a man born and educated in France, who lived while writing it in New York, but who referred to himself as a Pennsylvanian, and who stopped off in London, to arrange for the book's publication there, while he was on his way back to his native France—whence he would soon return to America as French consul in New

York where (as he told his friend Benjamin Franklin) he enjoyed "The Privileges of double citizenship."

I have deliberately emphasized the mix-up of tradition in Hector St. John de Crèvecoeur's background because I want to suggest that, in a sense, the American self-consciousness about his Americanness is still—as it was in 1782—in great part the result of a feeling or sense of "double citizenship." We Americans are all, in one way or another, aware of a double or bifurcated heritage. The eleventh-generation descendant of immigrants from Holland and the second-generation descendant of immigrants from China are no different in this respect from the eleventh-generation descendant of Negro slaves imported from the Congo. Each of us is conscious of a heritage as an American, and each of us is conscious of another heritage—or, more commonly, of a complex mixture of heritages—from cultures whose values are, in varying degrees, unlike those we have acquired as Americans.

In some sense this is no doubt true of other peoples as well as Americans. One thinks of the Canadians and Australians, for example, or the Liberians or the Israelis. Canada, with its bilingual culture, presents a special problem. It lives with a clear-cut, external duality between English-speaking Canadians and French Canadians, a cleavage which is marked by geographical as well as linguistic boundaries. But in so far as the French Canadian has been cut off from his French heritage, he was cut off from it by the Englishmen who have become his fellow Canadians, not by an act of his own will. Neither the English-speaking nor the French Canadians, nor the Australians, have voluntarily shattered the continuity of their non-Canadian or non-Australian heritage by an appeal to revolutionary violence, with its inevitable aftermath of resentment and passionate self-assertion.

As for the Liberians and Israelis, however diverse their national origins may be, their motive in immigrating to the countries in which they now live was to re-establish their ties to a heritage even older and more deeply rooted in them than that of the nation from which they came. The immigrant to the United States, however, has always been required (or has deliberately sought) to attach himself to a heritage-in-the-making—a heritage which is not in any sense one to which he is entitled by his ancestry, but one to whose shaping he, as much as (but no more than) anyone else, has the right and duty to contribute.

What James Baldwin, the American novelist, once said of the American Negro can be said with some justice of the white American as well: he arrives at his identity "by virtue of the absoluteness of his estrangement from his past." We Americans do, of course, nourish illusions of recovering the European or African or Asian or American-Indian half of our dual heritage. Some of us even maintain an illusory sort of psychologically dual citizenship. Such illusions may, indeed, be necessary as long as men are uncertain about the legitimacy of their status, and the American—white or non-white—has never been quite sure what his status is. For we are all, as it were, the younger sons, the disinherited, the bastard offspring of the past. The American estate to which we lay claim is not, and cannot be, ours by right of primogeniture. It is ours only by squatters' right, or by virtue of conquest or piracy or love.

For all these reasons it is true, I think, that the citizens of no other major world power share the special sense of "double citizenship" which from Crèvecoeur's time to ours has made the Americans so self-consciously inquisitive about "What is an American?" A century after Crèvecoeur, Henry James, one of the greatest American novelists, devoted his major energies to the imaginative exploration of the implications of that question, and entitled one of his major novels *The American*. I do not know of (and cannot imagine) any important French author writing a novel called *The Frenchman,* or any Russian writing one called *The Russian.* Our libraries are full of disputatious writings by Americans with titles like *The American Spirit in Art* and *The American Style in Politics*. There *is,* of course, a book called *The Englishness of English Art*—but it was not written by an Englishman, I assure you. Until recently, at least, the English have confidently known what was English about England and therefore have not had to be self-conscious about it. But the Americans have never been sure what it was to be Americans—which is why, from the beginning, they have asserted so loudly and so inconclusively that they *were* sure. I have a shelfful of books purporting to define the American spirit or the American character and they offer as many different definitions as there are books—all mistaken definitions, too, except one (the one I wrote), and even that one strikes me as slightly tainted by its author's myopia.

Now, the reasons for dwelling at some length on this characteristic in remarks which are addressed to non-Americans is that if you are a visitor or temporary resident in the United States, you probably have some reason to want to understand what the "American spirit" is, or what the "American character's" characteristics are. If you are curious about such things, we will be delighted; and if, when you return to your homes, you write a book about us, telling your countrymen the truth about America, be sure to get the book published in this country, too. It will almost certainly be a best seller—especially if it is very critical and says disagreeable things about the "Snow Queen" frigidity of American women; the low, materialistic interests of American men (and their humble subservience to their womenfolk); the disparity between our professions of democratic equality and our economic and educational segregation of Negroes; our addiction to comic books and bottled pop; and the rest.

If you write a book giving the lowdown on America from a foreign observer's point of view, you will be in good company. Some very intelligent foreigners have written some very interesting books about us—ranging from the Frenchman De Tocqueville's great work on *Democracy in America*, down through Lord Bryce's study of the *American Commonwealth*, to the Swedish Gunnar Myrdal's *The American Dilemma*. Each of these was and is popular with American readers. But you don't have to be as judicious and encyclopedic as De Tocqueville, Bryce, and Myrdal to be a hit with us. You can be as intemperate as Mrs. Trollope, who flatly told her English countrymen in 1832 that she had discovered the Americans to be horrid: "I do not like their principles," she wrote, "I do not like their manners, I do not like their opinions." And for her courtesy we have rewarded her by buying up unnumbered editions of her book—which is still—after a hundred and twenty years—in print.

The Derogatory Stance

This appetite of ours for comment about us, abusive or judicious, may seem an endearing quality, especially if you are looking forward to getting substantial royalty checks from an American publisher, but you should be warned that from other points of view it might prove to be a trap.

Put it this way, to start with. Our appetite for criticism and analysis of America by foreigners is an aspect of our self-conscious interest in discovering what "an American" is, and this in turn is a symptom of our not knowing. Since we don't know, and wish very much that we did (our philanthropic foundations spend hundreds of thousands of dollars a year subsidizing studies of precisely this question), we love to listen to anyone who talks as if he knew. If he bases what he says on statistical studies and the paraphernalia of sociological research, so much the better. But if he spins it all out of his head, we don't mind that either.

Being an essentially modest people—or shall I say a people who by education and admonition have been taught that the architecture of Greece, and the Roman code of law, and the painting of Flanders and France, and the ethical wisdom of the Orient, and the poetry and drama of England are unsurpassed and unsurpassable, and that even in technology and science the basic work is all European and we have merely applied the principles ingeniously—being whatever you want to call this, a modest or fundamentally unself-assured people—we find it easier to believe the derogatory things about ourselves than the approving ones. We also find it easier to say the derogatory things—in fiction, drama, and the expressive arts in general.

Of course there was a time when we could (and did) say the self-approving things. But nobody but an ass could have taken us very seriously in our moods of slapping ourselves on the back, and—as a matter of fact—few people did take it seriously. It was too obviously a kind of whistling in the dark. Not even the writers who "made the eagle scream," as the saying was in the nineteenth century, took themselves seriously; often they were being intentionally funny and fooled nobody except humorless English travelers and some uncommonly stuffy politicians. (I am, of course, oversimplifying here—but it is generally true, I think, that whenever an American says anything very flattering about American civilization, he hastens to counteract it with something unflattering, in order to avoid what he feels would be an air of "I'm better than you," in order to "take himself down a peg.")

The result is that in serious writing about the nature and quality of the American experience, both fiction and non-fiction, whether written by foreigners or by Americans, you are likely to find more that is derogatory than that is approving. And most of what is approving can easily be discounted as ignorant, or superficial, or mere high spirits.

Furthermore—and this is the root of the difficulty, if one is really intent upon learning what

America means—it is very easy to mistake the significance of the literature which criticizes or rejects American culture for its bourgeois values, its materialism, its complacency, and so on. We are all quite likely to take such criticism at its face value, and thereby miss the point. We are likely either to praise it for its success in embodying values "superior" to America's standardized middle-class mediocrity, or, if we are in a chauvinistic or jingoistic mood, to damn it out of hand for its wrongheadedness.

The significance of a novel like Sinclair Lewis's *Babbitt* is, I believe, missed if you conclude from it either that Lewis was "un-American" because he disapproved of businessmen like Babbitt or that his book represents a set of values "superior" to (and therefore not characteristic of) the values of the civilization men like Babbitt had created in America. For Lewis was not writing as one who has descended from a "higher" plane to observe our civilization. He writes as one of us, who has seen—from a perspective which he assumes his fellow Americans can share— the inadequacies, the forlorn limitations of certain aspects of American life—aspects which his readers will reject just as he does. And of course he was right. His novel was a great popular success. His readers, most of whom were in business or commerce, saw in Babbitt some of the very things that they saw in themselves, and toward which they felt, like

Lewis, an odd mixture of sardonic amusement and of loyalty.

What I am trying to suggest is that, if a foreign reader concluded, from the quality of photographic, tape-recorded reality which Lewis's technique imparts to his novel, that Babbitt was the typical American businessman of the 1920's—and if he further concluded that, since American civilization is a business civilization, he could draw from the novel some conclusions about the inadequacies and forlorn limitations of the civilization itself, he would have run a serious risk. Hitler and his cohorts took such a risk, gambling that a nation of Babbitts would not rise to the challenge of Nazi domination of Europe. The leaders of other nations may make a similar mistake if they get the impression from our current non-fiction that we are a nation of juvenile delinquents or if they conclude from our young poets and novelists that our young people are beatniks. For Jack Kerouac and Ginsberg, like Lewis and Mencken in the twenties, do not quite signify what they appear to be saying. Their significance, I think, is that they are witnesses to the basic and never-ceasing drive within our culture to lift itself, to be dissatisfied with its limitations, to try—at whatever cost in self-distrust or self-reproach—to discover what, indeed, is an American.

Citizens of a New World

I am afraid I am beginning to sound apocalyptic, as if, like the cheap politician whom the nineteenth-century humorists burlesqued, I were about to make the American eagle scream. I hope that is not what I am about to do.

For what interests me about American civilization is that it is not—even in name—the civilization of the United States. As that name "American" suggests, it is something whose relevance is not confined in political boundaries. I know that we use it that way some of the time. I know that our neighbors in Latin America sometimes are hurt by what they assume to be our arrogance in speaking of ourselves as Americans; for geographically, they are as much Americans as we who live in the United States. But I like to think that at least some of the time we know this as well as they do, and that when we call ourselves Americans we are not implying that they are *not* Americans, but are—on the contrary—thinking of ourselves not merely as citizens of the United States but as people living in a New World. For in a very real sense we, like all people whose lives have felt the impact of the twin energies of democracy and technology, *are* living in a New World—not merely the hemispheric New World of the geographers, but the New World which the great seventeenth-century English physician, Sir Thomas

Browne, called "the America and untravelled parts of truth." Everyone who lives in *this* America, in *this* new and untraveled world, is as much concerned as are those of us who live in the United States to discover "What is an American?"

I am sure that I forget from time to time, as most of my fellow citizens forget, that this New World is not coextensive with my nation, or—more provincial still—with my precinct. I know that United States foreign policy is often not synonymous with a policy which would be genuinely American in the sense of that word I have tried to suggest. But our tendency to behave, much of the time, as citizens of the United States is as human and natural as it is for people in other lands to behave as citizens of Ghana or India or France. We cannot ignore, nor should non-Americans who wish to understand us ignore, the national heritage of the United States and the privileges and obligations of its citizens. But if I am not mistaken what we all really want to know is what Crèvecoeur wanted to know a century and three quarters ago: what is an American? And that question can be answered, I think, only when we discover that non-geographical "America" which is, in fact, the community in whose citizenship all our bifurcated heritages, our dual citizenships, are ultimately involved. We shall know "what is an American," I suspect, only when we know who is fit to be a citizen of the New World to whose dynamics and energies the United States has made large contributions, but which is being shaped by people in all lands where the influence of modern technology, and of a democratic faith in man's unexplored potentialities, have been felt. For America, in this sense, is still in the making—is still the New World to which mankind has for so many centuries been adventuring.

What's "American" about America*

* The first version of this essay was given as a lecture at the University of Colorado, August 3, 1954, and published in the *Colorado Quarterly*, Winter 1955. Later versions were read at Smith College and at the Columbia University Seminar on American Civilization. The present version is revised from one published in *Harper's Magazine*, July 1956.

THE DISCOVERY OF AMERICA has never been a more popular pastime than it is today. Scarcely a week goes by without someone's publishing a new book of travels in the bright continent. Magazines here and abroad provide a steady flow of articles by journalists, historians, sociologists, and philosophers who want to explain the United States to themselves, or to itself, or to others.

The discoverers of America have, of course, been describing their experiences ever since Captain John Smith wrote his first book about America almost three hundred and fifty years ago. But as Smith himself noted, not everyone "who hath bin at Virginia, understandeth or knows what Virginia is." Indeed, just a few years ago the Carnegie Corporation, which supports a number of college programs in American Studies, entitled its quarterly report "Who Knows America?" and went on to imply that nobody does, not even "our lawmakers, journalists, civic leaders, diplomats, teachers, and others."

There is, of course, the possibility that some of the writers who have explored, vicariously or in person, this country's past and present may have come

to understand or know what America really is. But
how is the lay inquirer to judge which accounts to
trust? Especially since most of the explorers seem
to have found not one but two or more antipodal
and irreconcilable Americas. The Americans, we are
convincingly told, are the most materialistic of
peoples, and, on the other hand, they are the most
idealistic; the most revolutionary, and, conversely,
the most conservative; the most rampantly individu-
alistic, and, simultaneously, the most gregarious and
herdlike; the most irreverent toward their elders,
and, contrariwise, the most abject worshipers of
"Mom." They have an unbridled admiration of everything big, from bulldozers to bosoms; and they are
in love with everything diminutive, from the "small
hotel" in the song to the "little woman" in the
kitchen.

Maybe, as Henry James thought when he wrote
The American Scene, it is simply that the country
is "too large for any human convenience," too diverse in geography and in blood strains to make
sense as any sort of unit. Whatever the reason, the
conflicting evidence turns up wherever you look,
and the observer has to content himself with some
sort of pluralistic conception. The philosopher San-
tayana's way out was to say that the American
mind was split in half, one half symbolized by the
skyscraper, the other by neat reproductions of Colonial mansions (with surreptitious modern conveniences). "The American will," he concluded, "in-

habits the skyscraper; the American intellect inherits the Colonial mansion." Mark Twain also defined the split in architectural terms, but more succinctly: American houses, he said, had Queen Anne fronts and Mary Ann behinds.

And yet, for all the contrarieties, there remains something which I think we all feel to be distinctively American, some quality or characteristic underlying the polarities which—as Henry James himself went on to say—makes the American way of doing things differ more from any other nation's way than the ways of any two other Western nations differ from each other.

I am aware of the risks in generalizing. And yet it would be silly, I am convinced, to assert that there are not certain things which are more American than others. Take the New York City skyline, for example—that ragged man-made Sierra at the eastern edge of the continent. Clearly, in the minds of immigrants and returning travelers, in the iconography of the admen who use it as a backdrop for the bourbon and airplane luggage they are selling, in the eyes of poets and of military strategists, it is one of the prime American symbols.

Let me start, then, with the Manhattan skyline and list a few things which occur to me as distinctively American. Then, when we have the list, let us see what, if anything, these things have in common. Here are a dozen items to consider:

1. The Manhattan skyline
2. The gridiron town plan
3. The skyscraper
4. The Model-T Ford
5. Jazz
6. The Constitution
7. Mark Twain's writing
8. Whitman's *Leaves of Grass*
9. Comic strips
10. Soap operas
11. Assembly-line production
12. Chewing gum

Here we have a round dozen artifacts which are, it seems to me, recognizably American, not likely to have been produced elsewhere. Granted that some of us take more pleasure in some of them than in others—that many people prefer soap opera to *Leaves of Grass* while others think Mark Twain's storytelling is less offensive than chewing gum—all twelve items are, I believe, widely held to be indigenous to our culture. The fact that many people in other lands like them too, and that some of them are nearly as acceptable overseas as they are here at home, does not in any way detract from their obviously American character. It merely serves to remind us that to be American does not mean to be inhuman—a fact which, in certain moods of self-criticism, we are inclined to forget.

What, then, is the "American" quality which these dozen items share? And what can that quality tell us about the character of our culture, about the nature of our civilization?

Skylines and Skyscrapers

Those engaged in discovering America often begin by discovering the Manhattan skyline, and here as well as elsewhere they discover apparently irreconcilable opposites. They notice at once that it doesn't make any sense, in human or aesthetic terms. It is the product of insane politics, greed, competitive ostentation, megalomania, the worship of false gods. Its by-products, in turn, are traffic jams, bad ventilation, noise, and all the other ills that metropolitan flesh is heir to. And the net result is, illogically enough, one of the most exaltedly beautiful things man has ever made.

Perhaps this paradoxical result will be less bewildering if we look for a moment at the formal and structural principles involved in the skyline. It may be helpful to consider the skyline as we might consider a lyric poem, or a novel, if we were trying to analyze its aesthetic quality.

Looked at in this way, it is clear that the total effect which we call "the Manhattan skyline" is made up of almost innumerable buildings, each in competition (for height, or glamour, or efficiency, or respectability) with all of the others. Each goes its own way, as it were, in a carnival of rugged architectural individualism. And yet—as witness the universal feeling of exaltation and aspiration which the skyline as a whole evokes—out of this irrational, unplanned, and often infuriating chaos, an unforeseen unity has evolved. No building ever built in New York was placed where it was, or shaped as it was, because it would contribute to the aesthetic effect of the skyline—lifting it here, giving it mass there, or lending a needed emphasis. Each was built, all those now under construction are being built, with no thought for their subordination to any overall effect.

What, then, makes possible the fluid and everchanging unity which does, in fact, exist? Quite simply, there are two things, both simple in themselves, which do the job. If they were not simple, they would not work; but they are, and they do.

One is the gridiron pattern of the city's streets —the same basic pattern which accounts for Denver, Houston, Little Rock, Birmingham, and almost any American town you can name, and the same pattern which, in the form of square townships, sections, and quarter sections, was imposed by the Ordinance of 1785 on an almost continental scale as what Wolfgang Langewiesche has called "a diagram of the idea of the Social Contract," a blueprint for a future society in which men would live each in his own domain, free and equal, each man's domain clearly divided from his neighbor's.

Whatever its shortcomings when compared with the "discontinuous patterns" of modern planned communities, this artificial geometric grid—imposed upon the land without regard to contours or any preconceived pattern of social zoning—had at least the quality of rational simplicity. The section lines, along which roads and fences run due north-south and due east-west, and which are so clearly visible from a plane over most of the U.S.A., make most of the nation exactly what an airplane pilot wants country to be: graph paper. As Langewiesche, the pilot, has said: "You can time your [plane's] shadow with a stop-watch across two lines, and get your exact speed. You can head the airplane down a section line and check your compass. But you hardly need a compass. You simply draw your course on the map and see what angle it makes. Then you cross the sections at the same angle. You can't miss. If you want to go exactly west, you get on a fence and follow it." And this simple gridiron pattern, mimicked in the city's streets, horizontally controls the spacing and arrangement of the isolated rectangular shafts which go to make up the skyline.

The other thing which holds the skyline's diversity together is the structural principle of the skyscraper. When we think of individual buildings, we tend to think of details of texture, color, and form, of surface ornamentation or the lack of it. But

A New York Skyline Reflected in the Façade of the United Nations Building. (Black and white print from a color transparency photographed by Ernst Haas, courtesy of Magnum Photos.)

Detail from "Map of the United States and Territories. Showing the Extent of Public Surveys," Theodore Franks, draughtsman, 1866. From *Report of the Commissioner of the General Land Office for the Year 1866,* Washington, 1867.

as elements in Manhattan's skyline, these things are of little consequence. What matters there is the vertical thrust, the motion upward; and that is the product of cage, or skeleton, construction in steel—a system of construction which is, in effect, merely a three-dimensional variant of the gridiron street plan, extending vertically instead of horizontally.

The aesthetics of cage, or skeleton, construction have never been fully analyzed, nor am I equipped to analyze them. But as a lay observer, I am struck by fundamental differences between the effect created by height in the RCA building at Rockefeller Center, for example, and the effect created by height in Chartres cathedral or in Giotto's campanile. In both the latter (as in all the great architecture of the past) proportion and symmetry, the relation of height to width, are constituent to the effect. One can say of a Gothic cathedral, this tower is too high; of a Romanesque dome, this is top-heavy. But there is nothing inherent in cage construction to invite such judgments. A true skyscraper like the RCA building could be eighteen or twenty stories taller, or ten or a dozen stories shorter, without changing its essential aesthetic effect. Once steel cage construction has passed a certain height, the effect of transactive upward motion has been established; from there on, the point at which you cut it off is arbitrary and makes no difference.

Those who are familiar with the history of the skyscraper will remember how slowly this fact was realized. Even Louis Sullivan—greatest of the early skyscraper architects—thought in terms of having to close off and climax the upward motion of the tall building with an "attic" or cornice which should be, in its outward expression, "specific and conclusive." His lesser contemporaries worked for years on the blind assumption that the proportion and symmetry of masonry architecture must be preserved in the new technique. If with the steel cage one could go higher than with load-bearing masonry walls, the old aesthetic effects could be counterfeited by dressing the façade as if one or more buildings had been piled on top of another—each retaining the illusion of being complete in itself. You can still see such buildings in New York: the first five stories perhaps a Greco-Roman temple, the next ten a neuter warehouse, and the final five or six an Aztec pyramid. That Aztec pyramid is simply a cheap and thoughtless equivalent of the more subtle Sullivan cornice. Both structures attempt to close and climax the upward thrust, to provide an effect similar to that of the *Katharsis* of Greek tragedy.

But the logic of cage construction requires no such climax. It has less to do with the inner logic of masonry forms than with that of the old Globe-Wernicke sectional bookcases, whose interchangeable units (with glass-flap fronts) anticipated by fifty years the modular unit systems of so-called modern furniture. Those bookcases were advertised in the nineties as "always complete but never finished"—a phrase which could with equal propriety have been applied to the Model-T Ford. Many of us remember with affection that admirably simple mechanism, forever susceptible to added gadgets or improved parts, each of which was interchangeable with what you already had.

Here, then, are the two things which serve to tie together the otherwise irrelevant components of the Manhattan skyline: the gridiron ground plan and the three-dimensional vertical grid of steel cage construction. And both of these are closely related to one another. Both are composed of simple and infinitely repeatable units.

The Structure of Jazz

It was the French architect, Le Corbusier, who described New York's skyline as "hot jazz in stone and steel." At first glance this may sound as if it were merely a slick updating of Schelling's "Architecture . . . is frozen music," but it is more than that if one thinks in terms of the structural principles we have been discussing and the structural principles of jazz.

Let me begin by making clear that I am using the term jazz in its broadest significant application. There are circumstances in which it is important to define the term with considerable precision, as when you are involved in discussion with a disciple of one of the many cults, orthodox or progressive, which devote themselves to some particular subspecies of jazz. But in our present context we need to focus upon what all the subspecies (Dixieland, Swing, Bop, or Progressive Jazz) have in common; in other words, we must neglect the by no means uninteresting qualities differentiating one from another, since it is what they have in common which can tell us most about the civilization which produced them.

There is no definition of jazz, academic or otherwise, which does not acknowledge that its essential ingredient is a particular kind of rhythm. Improvisation is also frequently mentioned as an essential; but even if it were true that jazz always involves improvisation, that would not distinguish it from a good deal of Western European music of the past. It is the distinctive rhythm which differentiates all types of jazz from all other music and which gives to all of its types a basic family resemblance.

It is not easy to define that distinctive rhythm. Winthrop Sargeant has described it as the product of two superimposed devices: syncopation and polyrhythm, both of which have the effect of constantly upsetting rhythmical expectations. Andre Hodeir, in his analytical study, *Jazz: Its Evolution and Essence*, speaks of "an alternation of syncopations and notes played on the beat," which "gives rise to a kind of expectation that is one of jazz's subtlest effects."

As you can readily hear, if you listen to any

jazz performance (whether of the Louis Armstrong, Benny Goodman, or Dave Brubeck variety), the rhythmical effect depends upon there being a clearly defined basic rhythmic pattern to enforce the expectations which are to be upset. That basic pattern is the 4/4 or 2/4 beat underlying all jazz. Hence the importance of the percussive instruments in jazz: the drums, the guitar or banjo, the bull fiddle, the piano. Hence too the insistent thump, thump, thump, thump which is so boring when you only half-hear jazz—either because you are too far away, across the lake or in the next room, or simply because you will not listen attentively. But hence also the delight, the subtle effects good jazz provides as the melodic phrases evade, anticipate, and return to, and then again evade the steady basic four-beat pulse which persists, implicitly or explicitly, throughout the performance.

In other words, the structure of a jazz performance is, like that of the New York skyline, a tension of cross-purposes. In jazz at its characteristic best, each player seems to be—and has the sense of being—on his own. Each goes his own way, inventing rhythmic and melodic patterns which, superficially, seem to have as little relevance to one another as the United Nations building does to the Empire State. And yet the outcome is a dazzlingly precise creative unity.

In jazz that unity of effect is, of course, the result of the very thing each of the players is flouting: namely, the basic 4/4 beat—that simple rhythmic gridiron of identical and infinitely extendible units which holds the performance together. As Louis Armstrong once wrote, you would expect that if every man in a band "had his own way and could play as he wanted, all you would get would be a lot of jumbled-up, crazy noise." But, as he goes on to say, that does not happen, because the players know "by ear and sheer musical instinct" just when to leave the underlying pattern and when to get back on it.

What it adds up to, as I have argued elsewhere, is that jazz is the first art form to give full expression to Emerson's ideal of a union which is perfect only "when all the uniters are isolated." That Emerson's ideal is deeply rooted in our national experience need not be argued. Frederick Jackson Turner quotes a letter written by a frontier settler to friends back East, which in simple, unself-conscious words expresses the same reconciling of opposites. "It is a universal rule here," the frontiersman wrote, "to help one another, each one keeping an eye single to his own business."

One need only remember that the Constitution itself, by providing for a federation of separate units, became the infinitely extendible framework for the process of reconciling liberty and unity over vast areas and conflicting interests. Its seven brief articles, providing for checks and balances between interests, classes, and branches of the government, establish, in effect, the underlying beat which gives momentum and direction to a political process Richard Hofstadter has called "a harmonious system of mutual frustration"—a description that fits a jazz performance as well as it fits our politics.

The aesthetic effects of jazz, as Winthrop Sargeant long ago suggested, have as little to do with symmetry and proportion as have those of a skyscraper. Like the skyscraper, the total jazz performance does not build to an organically required climax; it can simply cease. The "piece" which the musicians are playing may, and often does, have a rudimentary Aristotelian pattern of beginning, middle, and end; but the jazz performance need not. In traditional Western European music, themes are developed. In jazz they are toyed with and dismantled. There is no inherent reason why the jazz performance should not continue for another 12 or 16 or 24 or 32 measures (for these are the rhythmic cages in jazz corresponding to the cages of a steel skeleton in architecture). As in the skyscraper, the aesthetic effect is one of motion, in this case horizontal rather than vertical.

Jazz rhythms create what can only be called momentum. When the rhythm of one voice (say the trumpet, off on a rhythmic and melodic excursion) lags behind the underlying beat, its four-beat measure carries over beyond the end of the underlying beat's measure into the succeeding one, which

From a painting by Jay Robinson (courtesy of the artist).

has already begun. Conversely, when the trumpet anticipates the beat, it starts a new measure before the steady underlying beat has ended one. And the result is an exhilarating forward motion which the jazz trumpeter Wingy Manone once described as "feeling an increase in tempo though you're still playing at the same tempo." Hence the importance in jazz of timing, and hence the delight and amusement of the so-called "break," in which the basic 4/4 beat ceases and a soloist goes off on a flight of fancy which nevertheless comes back surprisingly and unerringly to encounter the beat precisely where it would have been if it had kept going.

Once the momentum is established, it can continue until—after an interval dictated by some such external factor as the conventional length of phonograph records or the endurance of dancers—it stops. ("No stopping," as the signs on the thruways and parkways have it, "except for repairs.") And as if to guard against any Aristotelian misconceptions about an end, it is likely to stop on an unresolved chord, so that harmonically, as well as rhythmically, everything is left up in the air. Even the various coda-like devices employed by jazz performers at dances, such as the corny old "without a shirt" phrase of blessed memory, are often harmonically unresolved. They are merely conventional ways of saying "we quit," not, like Beethoven's insistent codas, ways of saying, "There now; that ties off all the loose ends;

I'm going to stop now; done; finished; concluded; signed, sealed, delivered."

We think of jazz as a twentieth-century phenomenon, and it is true that it did not emerge as a national music until after the First World War. But there are close (and unexplored) analogies between jazz and other forms of popular arts which have deep roots in our national life. One is the nineteenth-century minstrel show. Constance Rourke gives a vivid description of it in her classic work on *American Humor:*

> Endmen and interlocutors spun out their talk with an air of improvisation. . . . In the dancing a strong individualism appeared, and the single dancer might perform his feats on a peck measure, and dancers might be matched against each other with high careerings which belonged to each one alone; but these excursions were caught within the broad effect. Beneath them all ran the deep insurgence of the Negro choruses . . . and the choral dancing of the walk-around made a resonant primitive groundwork.

Here we have several analogies with the structure of jazz—especially the improvisatory manner and the individual flights of fancy and fantasy held together by a rhythmic groundwork (the 4/4 beat of the walk-around). And there are other ways in which jazz is related to the minstrel show. The min-

strel characters—Jim Crow, Zip Coon, Dan Tucker—
were blackface creations, and many jazz musicians,
both white and Negro, perpetuate the atmosphere
of burnt-cork masquerade.

Related to these analogies are those between
the form of jazz and the form of the humorous monologue, the dominant form in the tradition of American humor, from Seba Smith's Major Jack Downing
to Mark Twain and Mr. Dooley and on down to the
TV and night-club entertainers of our own time. In
these humorous monologues the apparent "subject"
is of as little importance as is the tune from which
a jazz performance takes off. It is the "talking
around" the subject without hitting it, the digress-
ing and ramifying, which matters.

Twain and Whitman

Since Mark Twain is the acknowledged master
of the humorous monologue in our literature, let us
look at an example of his work. His writing was, of
course, very largely the product of oral influences.
He was a born storyteller, and he always insisted
that the oral form of the humorous story was high
art. Its essential tool (or weapon), he said, is the
pause—which is to say, timing. "If the pause is too
long the impressive point is passed," he wrote, "and
the audience have had time to divine that a surprise
is intended—and then you can't surprise them, of

course." In other words, he saw the pause as a device for upsetting expectations, like the jazz "break."

Mark, as you know, was by no means a formal perfectionist. In fact he took delight in being irreverent about literary form. Take, for example, his account of the way *Pudd'nhead Wilson* came into being. It started out to be a story called "Those Extraordinary Twins," about a youthful freak consisting, he said, of "a combination consisting of two heads and four arms joined to a single body and a single pair of legs—and I thought I would write an extravagantly fantastic little story with this freak of nature for hero—or heroes—a silly young Miss [named Rowena] for heroine, and two old ladies and two boys for the minor parts."

But as he got writing the tale, it kept spreading along and other people began intruding themselves —among them Pudd'nhead, and a woman named Roxana, and a young fellow named Tom Driscoll, who before the book was half finished had taken things almost entirely into their own hands and were "working the whole tale as a private venture of their own."

From this point, I want to quote Mark directly, because in the process of making fun of fiction's formal conventions he employs a technique which is the verbal equivalent of the jazz "break"—a technique of which he was a master.

When the book was finished and I came to look round to see what had become of the team I had originally started out with—Aunt Patsy Cooper, Aunt Betsy Hale, the two boys, and Rowena the light-weight heroine—they were nowhere to be seen; they had disappeared from the story some time or other. I hunted about and found them—found them stranded, idle, forgotten, and permanently useless. It was very awkward. It was awkward all around, but more particularly in the case of Rowena, because there was a love match on, between her and one of the twins that constituted the freak, and I had worked it up to a blistering heat and thrown in a quite dramatic love quarrel, [now watch Mark take off like a jazz trumpeter flying off on his own in a fantastic break] wherein Rowena scathingly denounced her betrothed for getting drunk, and scoffed at his explanation of how it had happened, and wouldn't listen to it, and had driven him from her in the usual "forever" way; and now here she sat crying and broken-hearted; for she had found that he had spoken only the truth; that it was not he, but the other half of the freak that had drunk the liquor that made him drunk; that her half was a prohibitionist and had never drunk a drop in his life, and although tight as a brick three days in the week, was wholly innocent of blame; and indeed, when sober, was constantly doing all he could to reform his brother, the other half, who

never got any satisfaction out of drinking, anyway, because liquor never affected him. [Now
he's going to get back on the basic beat again.]
Yes, here she was, stranded with that deep in-
justice of hers torturing her poor torn heart.

Mark didn't know what to do with her. He couldn't
just leave her there, of course, after making such a
to-do over her; he'd have to account to the reader
for her somehow. So he finally decided that all he
could do was "give her the grand bounce." It
grieved him, because he'd come to like her after a
fashion, "notwithstanding she was such an ass and
said such stupid, irritating things and was so nause-
atingly sentimental"; but it had to be done. So he
started Chapter Seventeen with: "Rowena went out
in the back yard after supper to see the fireworks
and fell down the well and got drowned."

It seemed abrupt [Mark went on], but I
thought maybe the reader wouldn't notice it,
because I changed the subject right away to
something else. Anyway it loosened up Rowena
from where she was stuck and got her out of the
way, and that was the main thing. It seemed a
prompt good way of weeding out people that
had got stalled, and a plenty good enough way
for those others; so I hunted up the two boys
and said "they went out back one night to stone
the cat and fell down the well and got drowned."
Next I searched around and found old Aunt Patsy

> Cooper and Aunt Betsy Hale where they were aground, and said "they went out back one night to visit the sick and fell down the well and got drowned." I was going to drown some of the others, but I gave up the idea, partly because I believed that if I kept that up it would arouse attention, . . . and partly because it was not a large well and would not hold any more anyway.

That was a long excursion—but it makes the point: that Mark didn't have much reverence for conventional story structure. Even his greatest book, which is perhaps also the greatest book written on this continent—*Huckleberry Finn*—is troublesome. One can scarcely find a criticism of the book which does not object, for instance, to the final episodes, in which Tom rejoins Huck and they go through that burlesque business of "freeing" the old Negro Jim— who is, it turns out, already free. But, as T. S. Eliot was, I think, the first to observe, the real structure of *Huck Finn* has nothing to do with the traditional form of the novel—with exposition, climax, and resolution. Its structure is like that of the great river itself—without beginning and without end. Its structural units, or "cages," are the episodes of which it is composed. Its momentum is that of the tension between the river's steady flow and the eccentric superimposed rhythms of Huck's flights from, and near recapture by, the restricting forces of routine and convention.

It is not a novel of escape; if it were, it would be Jim's novel, not Huck's. Huck is free at the start, and still free at the end. Looked at in this way, it is clear that *Huckleberry Finn* has as little need of a "conclusion" as has a skyscraper or a jazz performance. Questions of proportion and symmetry are as irrelevant to its structure as they are to the total effect of the New York skyline.

There is not room here for more than brief reference to the other "literary" items on our list: Whitman's *Leaves of Grass*, comic strips, and soap opera. Perhaps it is enough to remind you that *Leaves of Grass* has discomfited many a critic by its lack of symmetry and proportion, and that Whitman himself insisted: "I round and finish little, if anything; and could not, consistently with my scheme." As for the words of true poems, Whitman said in the "Song of the Answerer"—

They bring none to his or her terminus or to be
    content and full,
Whom they take they take into space to behold the
    birth of stars, to learn one of the meanings,
To launch off with absolute faith, to sweep through
    the ceaseless rings and never be quiet again.

Although this is not the place for a detailed analysis of Whitman's verse techniques, it is worth noting in passing how the rhythm of these lines reinforces their logical meaning. The basic rhythmical unit, throughout, is a three-beat phrase of which there are two in the first line (accents falling on *none, his,* and *term . . . be, tent,* and *full*), three in the second (*take, take,* and *space . . . hold, birth, stars . . . learn, one, mean*), and three in the third (*launch, ab, faith . . . sweep, cease, rings . . . nev. qui, gain*).

Superimposed upon the basic three-beat measure there is a flexible, non-metrical rhythm of colloquial phrasing. That rhythm is controlled in part by the visual effect of the arrangement in long lines, to each of which the reader tends to give equal duration, and in part by the punctuation within the lines. For example, the comma pause after the second three-beat measure in line two (after *stars*) tends, since the first line consisted of two such measures, to establish an expectation of rest which is upset by the line's continuing for another measure. Then, in the final line, the placement of the comma pause reverses the pattern, requiring a rest after the first measure and doubling up the remaining two.

It is the tension between the flexible, superimposed rhythm of the rhetorical patterns and the basic three-beat measure of the underlying framework which unites with the imagery and the logical meaning of the words to give the passage its restless, sweeping movement. It is this tension and other analogous aspects of the structure of *Leaves of Grass* which give to the book that "vista" Whitman himself claimed for it.

If I may apply to it T. S. Eliot's idea about *Huckleberry Finn,* the structure of the *Leaves* is open at the end. Its key poem may well be the "Song of the Open Road," as D. H. Lawrence believed. "Toward no goal," Lawrence wrote. "Always the open road. Having no direction even. . . . This was Whitman. And the true rhythm of the American continent speaking out in him."

As for the comics and soap opera, they too—on their own frequently humdrum level—have devised structures which provide for no ultimate climax, which come to no end demanded by symmetry or proportion. In them both there is a shift in interest away from the "How does it come out?" of traditional storytelling to "How are things going?" In a typical installment of Harold Gray's *Little Orphan Annie,* the final panel shows Annie walking purposefully down a path with her dog, Sandy, saying: "But if we're goin', why horse around? It's a fine night for walkin' . . . C'mon, Sandy . . . Let's go . . ." (It doesn't even end with a period, or full stop, but with the conventional three dots or suspension points, to indicate incompletion.) So too, in the soap operas, *Portia Faces Life,* in one form or another, day after day, over and over again. And the operative word is the verb "faces." It is the process of facing that matters.

America Is Process

Here, I think, we are approaching the central quality which all the diverse items on our list have in common. That quality I would define as a concern with process rather than product—or, to re-use Mark Twain's words, a concern with the manner of handling experience or materials rather than with the experience or materials themselves. Emerson, a century ago, was fascinated by the way "becoming somewhat else is the perpetual game of nature." The universe, he said, "exists only in transit," and man is great "not in his goals but in his transitions."

This preoccupation with process is, of course, basic to modern science. "Matter" itself is no longer to be thought of as something fixed, but fluid and ever-changing. The modern sciences, as Veblen observed forty years ago, cluster about the "notion of process," the notion of "a sequence, or complex, of consecutive change." Similarly, modern economic theory has abandoned the "static equilibrium" analysis of the neo-classic economists, and in philosophy John Dewey's instrumentalism abandoned the classic philosophical interest in final causes for a scientific interest in the "mechanism of occurrences"—that is, process.

It is obvious, I think, that the American system of industrial mass production reflects this same focus of interest in its concern with production rather than products. And it is the mass-production system, *not* machinery, which has been America's contribution to industry.

In that system there is an emphasis different from that characteristic of handicraft production or even of machine manufacture. In both of these there was an almost total disregard of the means of production. The aristocratic ideal inevitably relegated interest in the means exclusively to anonymous peasants and slaves; what mattered to those who controlled and administered production was, quite simply, the finished product. In a mass-production system, on the other hand, it is the process of production itself which becomes the center of interest, rather than the product.

If we are aware of this fact, we usually regard it as a misfortune. We hear a lot, for instance, of the notion that our system "dehumanizes" the worker, turning him into a machine and depriving him of the satisfactions of finishing anything, since he performs only some repetitive operation. It is true that the unit of work in mass production is not a product but an operation. But the development of the system, in contrast with Charlie Chaplin's wonderful but wild fantasy of the assembly line, has shown the intermediacy of the stage in which the worker is doomed to frustrating boredom. Merely repetitive work, in the logic of mass production, can and must be done by machine. It is unskilled work which is doomed by it, not the worker. More and more skilled workers are needed to design products, analyze jobs, cut patterns, attend complicated machines, and co-ordinate the processes which comprise the productive system.

The skills required for these jobs are different, of course, from those required to make handmade boots or to carve stone ornament, but they are not in themselves less interesting or less human. Operating a crane in a steel mill, or a turret lathe, is an infinitely more varied and stimulating job than shaping boots day after day by hand. A recent study of a group of workers on an automobile assembly line makes it clear that many of the men object, for a variety of reasons, to those monotonous, repetitive jobs which (as we have already noted) should be—but in many cases are not yet—done by machine; but those who *like* such jobs like them because they enjoy the process. As one of them said: "Repeating the same thing you can catch up and keep ahead of yourself . . . you can get in the swing of it." The report of members of a team of British workers who visited twenty American steel foundries in 1949 includes this description of the technique of "snatching" a steel casting with a magnet, maneuvered by a gantry crane running on overhead rails:

> In its operation, the crane approaches a pile of castings at high speed with the magnet hanging fairly near floor level. The crane comes to a stop somewhere short of the castings, while the mag-

net swings forward over the pile, is dropped on to it, current switched on, and the hoist begun, at the same moment as the crane starts on its return journey. [And then, in words which might equally be applied to a jazz musician, the report adds:] The whole operation requires timing of a high order, and the impression gained is that the crane drivers derive a good deal of satisfaction from the swinging rhythm of the process.

This fascination with process has possessed Americans ever since Oliver Evans in 1785 created the first wholly automatic factory: a flour mill in Delaware in which mechanical conveyors—belt conveyors, bucket conveyors, screw conveyors—are interlinked with machines in a continuous process of production. But even if there were no other visible sign of the national preoccupation with process, it would be enough to point out that it was an American who invented chewing gum (in 1869) and that it is the Americans who have spread it—in all senses of the verb—throughout the world. A non-consumable confection, its sole appeal is the process of chewing it.

The apprehensions which many people feel about a civilization absorbed with process—about its mobility and wastefulness as well as about the "dehumanizing" effects of its jobs—derive, I suppose, from old habit and the persistence of values and tastes which were indigenous to a very different social and economic system. Whitman pointed out in *Democratic Vistas* ninety years ago that America was a stranger in her own house, that many of our social institutions, like our theories of literature and art, had been taken over almost without change from a culture which was not, as ours is, the product of political democracy and the machine. Those institutions and theories, and the values implicit in them, are still around, though some (like collegiate gothic, of both the architectural and intellectual variety) are less widely admired than formerly.

Change, or the process of consecutive occurrences, is, we tend to feel, a bewildering and confusing and lonely thing. All of us, in some moods, feel the "preference for the stable over the precarious and uncompleted" which, as John Dewey recognized, tempts philosophers to posit their absolutes. We talk fondly of the need for roots—as if man were a vegetable, not an animal with legs whose distinction it is that he can move and "get on with it." We would do well to make ourselves more familiar with the idea that the process of development is universal, that it is "the form and order of nature." As Lancelot Law Whyte has said, in *The Next Development in Man*:

> Man shares the special form of the universal formative process which is common to all organisms, and herein lies the root of his unity with the rest of organic nature. While life is main-

tained, the component processes in man never attain the relative isolation and static perfection of inorganic processes . . . The individual may seek, or believe that he seeks, independence, permanence, or perfection, but that is only through his failure to recognize and accept his actual situation.

As an "organic system" man cannot, of course, expect to achieve stability or permanent harmony, though he can create (and in the great arts of the past, has created) the illusion of them. What he can achieve is a continuing development in response to his environment. The factor which gives vitality to all the component processes in the individual and in society is "not permanence but development."

To say this is not to deny the past. It is simply to recognize that for a variety of reasons people living in America have, on the whole, been better able to relish process than those who have lived under the imposing shadow of the arts and institutions which Western man created in his tragic search for permanence and perfection—for a "closed system." They find it easy to understand what that very American philosopher William James meant when he told his sister that his house in Chocorua, New Hampshire, was "the most delightful house you ever saw; it has fourteen doors, all opening outwards." They are used to living in grid-patterned cities and towns whose streets, as Jean-Paul Sartre observed, are not, like those of European cities, "closed at both ends." As Sartre says in his essay on New York, the long straight streets and avenues of a gridiron city do not permit the buildings to "cluster like sheep" and protect one against the sense of space. "They are not sober little walks closed in between houses, but national highways. The moment you set foot on one of them, you understand that it has to go on to Boston or Chicago."

So, too, the past of those who live in the United States, like their future, is open-ended. It does not, like the past of most other people, extend downward into the soil out of which their immediate community or neighborhood has grown. It extends laterally backward across the plains, the mountains, or the sea to somewhere else, just as their future may at any moment lead them down the open road, the endless-vistaed street.

Our history is the process of motion into and out of cities; of westering and the counter-process of return; of motion up and down the social ladder— a long, complex, and sometimes terrifyingly rapid sequence of consecutive change. And it is this sequence, and the attitudes and habits and forms which it has bred, to which the term "America" really refers.

"America" is not a synonym for the United States. It is not an artifact. It is not a fixed and immutable ideal toward which citizens of this nation strive. It has not order or proportion, but neither is it chaos except as that is chaotic whose components no single mind can comprehend or control. America is process. And in so far as Americans have been "American"—as distinguished from being (as most of us, in at least some of our activities, have been) mere carriers of transplanted cultural traditions— the concern with process has been reflected in the work of their heads and hearts and hands.

The Curriculum
of Discovery*

* This essay is revised from an address given at the commencement exercises, Rhode Island School of Design, June 2, 1956, and subsequently published by the college in pamphlet form.

HERE IS A JOKE from a recent issue of a college magazine. A prospective employer says to a job applicant, "Yes, I'll give you a job. Sweep out the store." "But I'm a college graduate!" the young man protests. "Okay," comes the withering reply, "I'll show you how."

There it is: the distrust of non-technical, non-practical education. It is still around, even in these days of national concern about aid to higher education. It lurks in the background of much of the lip service paid to the "liberal arts" as opposed to "vocational" courses. And not without reason.

A century ago an almost impassable chasm existed between the interests and values of the everyday world of work and those of higher education as epitomized by the liberal arts. But there were increasing numbers of men of affairs and educators who saw, from their antipodal points of view, that the split was disastrous. On every hand there were demands that education must become more practical, meaning more immediately relevant to the concerns of an industrial society. Charles W. Eliot was about to re-orient Harvard's curriculum in ways which were to have widespread effects throughout our educational system, introducing new subjects in the curriculum and loosening the old "classical" bonds. At about the same time separate institutions for advanced scientific and technical training, such as M.I.T. (where Eliot had taught before he went to Harvard) and the Rhode Island School of Design, were founded on the theory that no amount of juggling with the traditional curriculum would suffice for the training of men and women competent to deal with the highly specialized techniques and processes of modern civilization.

As a result of all this, the sum total of higher education became more closely related to the world of business and industry than it had been, but within education itself the split between "practical" and "cultural" studies remained. Indeed, in many instances these distinct aspects of learning became the province of separate institutions, as with the Sheffield Scientific School and Yale. Where both did manage to exist under the same roof, they were uneasy collaborators, full of mutual suspicion and distrust. In spite of appearances, the chasm between industry and culture was as wide and as deep as ever.

Looking back on it now, we can see that in a society which dissociates the technical and humane skills, both suffer. We know that in Europe and America, the practical world tended for more than a century to depend too exclusively upon technical skills, with the result that business and industry and the spheres of life they dominated were in a measure dehumanized. What we less often recognize is that the world of culture, on the other hand, shunning the new environment of man's workaday life, turned in upon itself, marrying itself to its own past. And the more it did so, the more anemic and impotent it became.

If the symbol of one of these worlds became the "satanic mills," the symbol of the other became the mortuary grandeur of the museum. And in the field of education it was the liberal-arts curriculum which too often became a museum, as grand as it was inanimate.

In our lifetimes, events have made it impossible for the scholar and artist to maintain their isolation from the industrial and technical environment, or for the "practical" man to ignore the problem of values which are the province of liberal arts when they are alive and procreative. Much has been done in recent years to bridge the gap which had widened during the preceding century; but bridging a gap and closing it are not the same thing, and in that respect much remains to be done.

The Erudite Outsiders

When those trained in the liberal arts and humanities first began to turn their attention sympathetically to the problems and potentialities of modern industrial civilization, they were handicapped by the fact that they were outsiders looking in. Their interest and their rapidly increasing knowledge tended to be theoretical. It was not founded upon what William James called "knowledge of acquaintance"—that is, knowledge derived from firsthand experience of a situation or a fact. What they proceeded to build up, therefore, in such fields of study as sociology, economics, and even in such fields as artistic and literary criticism, was "knowledge about" the dynamic areas of modern life, or erudition: the kind of knowledge that is derived not from firsthand experience but from reflection and abstract reasoning.

Both knowledge-of-acquaintance and knowledge-about are essential for the educated man or woman. Neither is in the long run adequate without the other. But knowledge of acquaintance—the empirical, practical kind—has at least this temporary advantage over the other: it can be put straight to work. Erudition, on the other hand, by itself, is often pragmatically useless, is mere words. In that simple fact lies the justification for that joke about the businessman's assuming that the college graduate wouldn't know how to cope with a broom.

The problem facing the educator is that though knowledge-of-acquaintance is not difficult to acquire, it is very difficult to teach. As Elton Mayo of the Harvard Business School pointed out some years ago, erudition can more easily be passed on to others than knowledge which depends upon trial and error, example and imitation. And that is one reason why the academic profession in general prefers erudition to the other kind of knowledge.

But the educator's prejudice in favor of erudition has other and deeper roots. To a degree few of us would now willingly acknowledge, our preference relates back to the old snobbishness with which cultivated people looked down upon the merely practical problems of business and trade. Notice, for example, that almost the only area of liberal-arts education where knowledge-of-acquaintance as well as erudition is insisted upon is in the sciences, which are the newest part of the liberal arts curriculum. In physics, chemistry, psychology, and so on, laboratory work goes hand in hand (as it should) with the fruits of reflection and abstract reasoning. In the older parts of the curriculum—in history, literature, and the older social studies—only tentative and experimental moves have been made toward devising effective equivalents of laboratory work.

The result is that, in the liberal arts and humanities, our colleges are still a long way from providing that kind of education which young people in our industrial civilization require and deserve if we expect them to provide leadership for it. Anyone who doubts this would do well to look at the results of a survey on higher education published in *Fortune* several years ago. A representative sample of American parents was asked why they wanted their sons and daughters to go to college, and what they wanted them to get out of it. The answer, both for sons and daughters, was overwhelmingly: preparation for a better job, or for a trade or profession; greater earning power. Only two per cent spoke of wanting their sons to get "culture, appreciation of the arts," and only four per cent wanted their daughters to get it.

There is a grim warning in this for those of us who think that it is to the liberal arts that men must look for that rounded development which may, under favorable circumstances, enable them to think logically and imaginatively, to understand their fellows and make themselves understood, to apply ideas to specific situations, and to make appropriate value judgments. It means that the pressures for getting on with the world's work still threaten to rob us of the time we need to consider the directions in which we want that work to take us. It is no wonder that, in a time when public opinion sets such high store by technical skill, the colleges find it so difficult to get financial support for work in humanities and the arts. We are in danger of forgetting that he who keeps his nose to the grindstone may get the immediate job done but may also grind away his nose, to spite his fate, if not his face.

Lest we become too despondent, however, there is another side to the picture. The leaders of industry and business—the practical men—are increasingly aware that technical skills without the humane skills to direct them are not adequate even for purely practical and limited ends. Not long ago a large engineering corporation made a survey of its key executives' educational backgrounds. It found (as any good liberal-arts professor could have prophesied it would) that few of them came from technical schools; one was an apostate divinity student, one an ex-vaudeville man, and the majority came from liberal-arts colleges. Graduates of technical schools were invaluable in subordinate posts, carrying on the specialized aspects of the corporation's work, but they rarely rose above that level.

The Deadly Routine of Mere Skill

From both sides of the chasm, then, the need for closing the gap between knowledge-of-acquaintance and knowledge-about is recognized. But what have the educators done in the face of such evidence? Too often the technical and vocational schools have simply added to their curricula a few courses in literature or history. Similarly, the liberal-arts colleges too often have merely added a few practical courses (like "Writing for the Radio" or "Business English" or "Applied Psychology"). What it amounts to is that the vocational institution tells its students that in addition to the "useful" courses they came to school to get, they must also take some useless ones. And the liberal-arts colleges, panic-stricken at the rise of vocationalism and envious of the largesse which industry and government distribute to encourage practical and technical training, tell the job-conscious student that if he will just come and submit peaceably to culture, they will slip him a few useful courses on the side. The net effect, of course, in both instances, is that the gap between the technical and humane skills remains about as wide as before.

No society, least of all an industrial one, can master its enemies—or itself—if it depends for leadership upon men and women who are lopsidedly trained. I would wholeheartedly agree with my Columbia colleague, Jacques Barzun, that it is extremely dangerous to have the control of an industrial civilization rest in the hands of technical experts, or as he describes them, "a large, powerful, and complacent class of college-trained uneducated men."

Just as fearful, however, would be the prospect of depending for leadership upon members of a select, self-confident class, so stuffed with the kind of erudition which an enfeebled liberal-arts tradition often imparts that they had only contempt for the values (including the aesthetic and moral values) inherent in industrial civilization. Yet it is this contempt—a systematically supercilious contempt— which a good deal of so-called liberal-arts education still, in spite of its high intentions, tends to produce.

A great deal, I think, depends upon people who

have experienced a blend, or compound, of both kinds of training. It is good to get practical and technical training, to have opportunities to gain knowledge-of-acquaintance. It is good, also, to have opportunities to look through some of the doors which are opened by the liberal arts, because in so far as we avail ourselves of those opportunities, we will find that we are free. Free from the deadly routine of mere proficiency and skill; free from the threat of obsolescence which inevitably accompanies any technique in a civilization as mobile and changing as the one in which it is our destiny and our opportunity to live.

We hear a great deal about the need for more experts, more technically trained specialists: engineers, nuclear physicists, and so on. Only by training such specialists, it is said, can we preserve and defend our civilization against its enemies. Maybe so; but I doubt it. Nations or individuals who commit themselves to specialized techniques, no matter how advanced those techniques may be, lock themselves into rigid assumptions and expectations which some more adaptable and more imaginative nation or individual will inevitably upset. Techniques, whether in warfare or the arts or industry, are the ruts left by imaginative activity and disciplined thought en route to doing something. As long as that something is worth doing again, the ruts are worth following. But the capacity to follow them has little to do with the capacity to determine when and for how long something is worth doing, or with the power to discover, among all the things that have never been done before, what is worth doing next.

Liberal Crafts and Illiberal Arts*

* This essay is a revision of a keynote address given at the third annual Conference of American Craftsmen, June 20, 1959. Part of it was published in the October 1959 issue of *Industrial Design*.

IMPLICIT IN MUCH THAT WE SAY, and in many of the things we make and do, there seems to be the assumption that whatever is wrong or disappointing about the industrial society in which we live can be cured, or at least ameliorated, by reviving or adapting the values we inherit from a reputedly happier time when society was based upon agriculture and handicraft commerce. In the field of education this assumption underlies a good deal of the pleading for more attention to the liberal arts. In our discussions of the material products of our culture, it underlies our glorification of craftsmanship as opposed to mass production.

Science and technology, upon which industrial production rests, are commonly thought of as at best neutral agents (atomic energy is neither good nor bad in itself; it is what the politicians or generals or doctors do with it that matters). At worst they are thought to be anti-human (the assembly line), tending inevitably to dwarf our individuality and reduce us all to mechanical fragments in an irrational chaos. Either way, science and technology look pretty scary, and a society based upon them is obviously in need of a good strong infusion of those time-tested values which the liberal arts and the handcrafts preserve and cultivate.

Much has been written in recent years about the role of education in preserving and fostering the heritage of the past, but less has been said about the contemporary interest in the crafts and in craftsmanship as a manifestation of a similar attitude toward the past. The concern with craftsmanship is obviously a significant feature of our time. Automobiles manufactured in plants which are the epitome of mass-production technology are advertised in terms which appeal to the buyer's admiration for the unique values of craftsmanship. The New York *Times* recently reported that a California company is doing a good business in little plaques to be attached to the dashboards of Plymouths and Pontiacs, which read: "Especially manufactured for . . ." with your name inserted. The term "artsy-crafty" may be a contemptuous epithet to fling at the non-functional and spuriously antique, but we speak of "the arts and crafts" with increasing respect.

Those who call themselves craftsmen seem to fall into two groups. There are the one-of-a-kind makers, who by and large avoid machines except those which, like the hand loom or the potter's wheel, are sufficiently ancient to have acquired non-industrial associations. And there are the craftsmen who design and make objects which may serve as models for production-line manufacture. Both groups appear to share the wish, or determination, to contribute to our industrial civilization certain values (or, more specifically, certain qualities of form and color and texture) which were evolved in pre-industrial society and whose loss—or neglect—would diminish our pleasures or, worse still, deprive us of perceptions which can enrich our lives. One group seeks to do this by reviving or carrying on the actual handcrafts, with all their qualities of uniqueness—making things and perpetuating processes in direct (and often successful) competition with the things and processes of industrial technology. The other group, in the spirit of missionaries to the industrial heathen, carries the gospel into the factories themselves and seeks to reshape the products of industrialism in the image of the crafts.

The assumption that we can learn from the past how to correct what is wrong in industrial society is, generally speaking, an article of faith among all sorts and conditions of men. One encounters it everywhere from the *Reader's Digest* to the *Partisan Review*, from editorials in the Chicago *Tribune* to the Harvard report on *General Education in a Free Society*. At a recent symposium on "The New View of Man" to which notable scholars in many fields contributed, a distinguished liberal-arts professor produced a paragraph which can serve as a characteristic sample of the spontaneous overflow of anti-technological emotion. He was talking about the split between the artist and society. And, like everyone else, he traced that split to the industrial revolution, which during the past century and a half has "mechanized our lives and our outlook." Perhaps out of deference to some of his faculty colleagues he conceded that science and technology had brought "immense gains" to mankind. But with that concession out of the way, he went on to say that we'd have to admit "that the old way of life [the pre-industrial way] was natural, and that life in the modern megalopolis is unnatural."

> A man and his family are no longer, even in the country, a self-sufficient community, living close to a stable tradition and the processes of nature, but are mobile, isolated, rootless atoms, dependent upon a multitude of external agencies. Unless he makes a determined effort, an effort that invites the label of eccentricity, modern man loses the use of his hands and his feet and his senses, not to mention the time and capacity for reflection.

In contrast with all this, he said, art "starts from the natural activity of man's natural faculties . . . its values are not the values of a mechanized, acquisitive society."

I have quoted at such length because the rhetoric of this passage fascinates me. The tune is so familiar we could all whistle it, once we have heard the opening measures. It is full of haunting phrases which remind us of one another, like the songs of our childhood: "self-sufficient community," "stable tradition," and "close to nature" (the slight variation on this last phrase, "close to the processes of nature," won't throw anyone off the tune), and, in a sort of simple counterpoint with these nostalgic bits, we hear "mobile, isolated, rootless," "loses the use of his hands and feet," and "no time for reflection." (I missed "frenetic hurry" and "robot" in this last sequence—but one can't have everything.)

Before we examine the paragraph further, I should, however, make clear that it is not typical of the essay from which I have extracted it. The essay deals thoughtfully with the role of literature and of the writer in our society, not with technology and science, and the author is a professor of literature, not a student of society or the history of technics. But that is precisely why this paragraph is useful to us here: it is a completely unself-conscious compendium of the clichés which leap to our tongues when we feel sentimental about the good old days of literature, art, and craftsmanship. As such, it is worth a look, to see if the assumptions underlying the clichés have any coherent relevance to the state of affairs in which we find ourselves.

Natural Arts and Unnatural Sciences

What does it mean to say that man's life in pre-industrial society was "natural," while the life of man today is not? Is it not "natural" for man to make tools, and to power those tools with machines, and to use those tools to remake his environment? What is "unnatural" about being mobile? Were we not born with legs and endowed by nature with minds capable of conceiving of the wheel and a motor to drive it? Is mobility on wheels less "natural" than mobility on legs, or only less brutish and more "human"? And what is unnatural about a rootless atom? Could there be anything more unnatural than an atom *with* roots? Are a man and his family who have television, a car, and a telephone really more "isolated" than those who herded sheep in Palestine two thousand years ago, or those who lived in eighteenth-century English country houses? Are stable traditions more natural than unstable ones? And are the processes of nature, to which we like to think of being close, really stable or, as Werner Heisenberg's "uncertainty principle" in modern physics suggests, at best relatively so? And isn't it curious that a society which has deprived all but the eccentric of the use of their feet and hands and senses, regularly cracks the four-minute mile, buys fishing rods and skis in unprecedented quantities, operates turret lathes and typewriters with dextrous grace, and has learned to respond creatively to sensory stimuli which, without the microscopes and X rays and other resources technology and science have put at our disposal, man would never have seen or felt or heard?

In short, are not all of these deprecatory comparisons of the "natural" life of the old days with

the "unnatural" life of our own society either meaningless or—worse—a sentimental refuge from thinking about the challenge which our society really of-
fers us? For there is a challenge involved, as there
always has been and always will be. Life attends to
that.

The paragraph ends by saying that since art
starts from "the natural activity of man's natural
faculties" its values have nothing in common with
those of our mechanized, acquisitive society. I hope
it is clear that in so far as this stereotyped conclusion
rests upon the notion that there is something unnatural about contemporary society, it is highly suspect. But there are two more points to be made.

The first is that, if the writer means what he
says, he is sounding the death knell of art. For he has
said that the values of art have no relevance to the
values of a "mechanized, acquisitive society" and
he has said that we are living in just such a society.
Society is us; if society's values are not those of art,
the values of art are not ours, and we can and will
dispense with it. That, in cold logic, is what the
paragraph says, but we would agree, I think, that it
is not what the author meant.

What did he mean? Or, to bring the problem
to our own doors, what do we mean when we say
things like that? We mean, I suppose, very little more
than that there are times when it seems that too
many people don't care enough about the things we
design or write or paint, or about those books or

paintings or other artistic achievements which have given joy and perceptive understanding to many people in the past and which still have the capacity to give such joy and understanding. Some of us are so anxious to coddle our pride in our lonely sensibility that when thirty million people watch *Hamlet* on TV some evening, we quickly find ways to belittle the fact. We point out that it was, after all, a capsule *Hamlet,* reduced to an hour and a half—as if that proved that the thirty million wouldn't have watched for two and a half or three hours if the producers had been able to afford or get the time. Of course it may be true that if the whole play, uncut, had been televised on a three-hour program, only fifteen or twenty million would have watched; but it is also true that there might have been thirty-five million. We can't be sure. What we can be sure of is that no comparable fraction of the total population of the English-speaking world ever deliberately exposed themselves to *Hamlet* in any "natural" state of society before the industrial revolution. It may be a pity that an even larger fraction of the possible TV audience watched other shows that night, instead. But even here I think we should be careful not to be too sure. Maybe what they were watching was worth watching. The chances are good, if Shakespeare's career means anything, that the profoundest and most enduring creative work of our time will be done —as his was—for a popular medium of entertainment. If it is, there is not much chance of its being seen, or appreciated, or encouraged by those of us who mourn the sorry fate of art in our mechanized, "unnatural" times. It often seems to me that if art needs any defending, it needs defending from those of us who call ourselves its friends; against its enemies, I am sure, it is quite capable of defending itself.

We do no one any good by indulging in sentimental stereotypes about the inferiority of our society to the societies of the past. We simply confuse ourselves, discourage the creative artists (if they take us seriously), and lead the general public to conclude (quite justifiably) that if art is, as we seem to find it comforting to think, something which only people like us can enjoy, we're welcome to it.

This brings me to the second and final point about the paragraph from which I have quoted. Toward the end of it, the author uses two terms to characterize our society. He calls it mechanized and acquisitive. At the beginning he had talked as if it was the mechanization introduced by science and technology which made industrial society at odds with the artist. Now, suddenly, a new element—acquisitiveness—is introduced, and introduced in such a way that it is made to seem like just another name for mechanization, as if a society which is mechanized is *ipso facto* acquisitive.

Those who remember Veblen's classic distinction between the acquisitive motives and the motives of production and service will have already detected the irony of this verbal juggling. For mechanization and acquisitiveness have nothing in common, and the values of a society based upon science and technology are in the profoundest sense at odds with those of an acquisitive society.

Is It Natural to Be Human?

We come face to face, at this point, with the basic challenge our society presents to us. Is it, in fact, a society whose values are primarily shaped by science and technology? To the extent that it is so, it is something new under the sun, and makes unprecedented demands upon those who do its work, direct its dynamic forces, and give artistic expression to its aspirations and doubts. If it is merely an acquisitive society, a business society rather than an industrial one, and if it is motivated primarily by the desire for power and pecuniary gain, there is nothing new about it. In that case it may well be true that the moral problems confronting the modern individual are essentially the same as those which have confronted individuals in the past, and that the insights and perceptions contained in the literature and art which have come down to us from the ancient East, and through the long tradition of Western culture, provide us with the most direct and powerful illumination of life's meaning and its potentialities.

The challenge society presents to us is the challenge to look about us, with minds and senses unclouded by stereotyped responses, and to think and speak and act in unhackneyed response to what we see. If we can accept this challenge, we may discover that the society we live in really is, as we frequently say it is but seldom believe it is, founded upon and shaped by technology and science. To the extent that it *is* so founded, it is a society which puts a premium upon adaptability, mobility, and a willingness to forego the security of fixed status and the certainty of dogmatic absolutes. For technology and science always and everywhere make for change. They are not mere collections of machines and test tubes, but processes by which we change our environment and thereby change ourselves. They are therefore the ineluctable enemies of all the static, traditional features of society as men knew it in the past—the enemies of all varieties of vested interest, of all the habitual and ceremonial aspects of institutions, of all fixed systems of dogma, whether the dogma be religious, political, or aesthetic.

It would be surprising indeed if, in such a society, the arts of the past, expressing very different values, should not in some important respects seem less relevant than they once seemed. And it would be still more surprising if the reputations of some artists, who once seemed of the first importance, should not dwindle while those of others (such as El Greco and Blake) should be enhanced.

Similarly, it would be inconceivable that the artists and craftsmen of our own time, whether they are working in traditional modes or in the new media which have been provided by technology itself, should not express in their creations those values which our society demands. For what society wants, society gets.

A society based upon science and technology wants artists and craftsmen and workers whose values are relevant to the type of interdependence which science and technology require of mankind. As Walt Whitman knew a century ago, the "American" world (whose boundaries, as I have suggested, are not by any means limited to those of the United States) demands a new individuality—an individuality freed from ceremonial homage to dead certainties and imaginatively responsive to the challenge of "a revolutionary and future-founding age."

Fifty years ago, Simon Patten, a pioneer of economics in America, delivered a series of lectures on *The New Basis of Civilization,* one of which concludes with a relevant passage. Science and technology, Patten said, had already, by 1905, "fundamentally altered" the elemental relations between man and nature which had formerly existed. To say that the methods which have made men physically independent of the local climate and the local food supply, which have given him control over nature in so many respects, are artificial or "unnatural," was, Patten said, to underrate the powers of technology and science "by implying that they are constantly opposed by fundamental natural forces which in the end must again triumph." The triumph of man's scientific and technical intelligence over the materials of nature was to Patten as "natural" as any other step in the evolution of life on earth.

> Each gain upon nature [he wrote] adds to the quantity of goods to be consumed by society and lessens the labor necessary to produce them. In one form the surplus is stored in individuals as surplus energy; in another it is in the goods produced by this energy. . . . The surplus is not conserved as a permanent fund, but exists and grows only as it is perpetually transformed from goods to energy and from energy back to goods. . . . It relieves the present from the menace of a deficit which our forefathers constantly faced and feared. As a concept of our social thinking it differentiates the new from the old and helps to drive away the mists that blur clear thinking.

Reading these words written in 1905, those of us who remember the great depression of the thirties, and the horrors of two world wars brought on in part by nations of men who feared "the menace of a deficit," may conclude that Patten was naïvely optimistic about the future of a society based upon man's scientific and technical mastery of nature's materials. Such a conclusion is unwarranted, unless we can demonstrate that it was the new bases of society which caused the depression and the wars, and this would be hard to demonstrate. Patten was by no means naïvely optimistic about the immediate future, and the wars would not have surprised him. The concept of surplus energy would, he said, "help to drive away the mists that blur clear thinking" about society and its possibilities, but as he promptly went on to say, "states of mind are hard to change, and in truth those we so long ago adopted seem to find ever fresh justification in the evils which remain to afflict men long after their inciting causes have disappeared; in the old wounds of humanity it is easy to see new proofs of accustomed beliefs."

> We know [he said] that the military state is gradually being displaced by the industrial state, and yet there never was a time when the power and efficiency of armies was as great as now. . . . And so it is with the evils more directly associated with the industrial world. The poverty, misery, exploitation, oppression of the poor; the greed, indifference, and power of the rich, are glaring truths even while the basis of a new economic order becomes more and more plain. In the age of transition the old thought and the new world abide side by side. But if the foundations of our civilization have been changed, the altering status of men will take clearer aspect in each new age, and the old thought, while apparently verifying the old

premises anew, will gradually disappear—not because it is argued away, but because men's sentiments are changed by new activity and an accumulating store of fresh experiences.

As a teacher, I know Patten was correct in saying that the old thought, the old states of mind, cannot be argued away. I know also that in great measure the educational system in which I play a part is still dominated by the values and states of mind of a time when men were under the domination of nature, and when it was therefore essential to train their hands to overcome, and their minds to transcend, the savagery of land and water. It is an education which, as Patten knew, "teaches that beauty is in medieval craftsmanship, and ugliness in the machine-made object," and which turns the student toward the abstractions of logic and the consolations of historical study in all fields.

I know also, that the great task of education, and the great challenge to artists and craftsmen, is to arouse man to the domination of his new, man-made environment—the urban world of the industrial megalopolis—"by stimulating eye and ear until he sees and hears fresh inducements to activity" and by making him acquainted with the unimagined possibilities of a world which, if strange, is strange only because we have not yet quite dared to believe that to be human in ways which control nature is quite natural to human beings.

Farewell, Architecture!*

SPECIALIZED ART
IN A VERNACULAR CULTURE

* This essay incorporates material from two earlier papers. Some of the material was originally written to be read before the Architecture Society of the Rhode Island School of Design, on November 3, 1958, and was published by the society in a pamphlet entitled *Whatever Became of Architecture?* Most of the rest is revised from the summation address at the First Pacific Rim Conference, sponsored by the California Council of the American Institute of Architects, held in Honolulu, Hawaii, October 8–14, 1959, and published in the *Architectural Record*, April 1960.

ARCHITECTURE SEEMS TO BE a flourishing art. New buildings are going up in all our cities. A number of architects are well-known figures, and most members of the profession appear to be prospering. But a diminishing fraction of our architecture is the work of architects. Most buildings are designed (if that isn't too flattering a term) by builders, contractors, engineers, or industrial designers. Even those which architects claim to have designed are frequently in large part the work of such specialists as the structural engineers, heating and ventilating engineers, acoustical engineers, interior designers, and the public relations and marketing experts with whom architects form partnerships or whom they employ.

What first called my attention sharply to the architect's diminishing role in architecture was some statements I came upon in the annual of the Society of Industrial Designers, *U. S. Industrial Design 1951*. In the section on "Commercial Interiors and Exteriors" it is casually asserted, without the least tone of surprise or triumph, that "in recent years the members of the Society of Industrial Designers have become increasingly active in certain fields that once were considered the exclusive province of the architect." In these activities they are serving not only their established clients but "many corporations which have not yet retained industrial designers for any other type of assignment."

The matter-of-fact tone in which this information is conveyed is, from the point of view of a layman interested in architecture, astonishing. But even more astonishing is the fact that, so far as I am able to discover, no architect and no architectural publication was astonished by it.

Why is it that industrial designers are increasingly being called upon to take over jobs formerly done by architects, even for clients who do not hire industrial designers to do what they are set up to do? Why have industrial designers, not architects, been asked to design not only ships, trains, and airplanes, but also theaters, service stations, retail shops, department stores, and corporate administration buildings? How does it happen that it was Raymond Loewy who got the job of designing Filene's largest branch store, or Walter Dorwin Teague who got the job of designing the first joint project ever undertaken by two major stores—the co-ordinated suburban stores of S. S. Pierce and R. H. Stearns in Chestnut Hill outside Boston, for which Teague designed and executed the entire complex, including plot-treatment, buildings, interiors, and fixtures?

The design annual's answer to these questions

is simply that none of these structures is primarily an architectural project. "Architecture here," it tells us, "is merely a technique of creating or enclosing a functional machine, and in each case the machine must be made efficient and attractive by exactly the same methods employed to make a manufactured product successful on the market." To the design of anything from a department store to a city, the industrial designer, we are told, applies exactly the same processes he is accustomed to apply in designing a refrigerator or an office machine. "It is precisely because [he] follows this unconventional procedure," according to the annual, "that he is now finding so many opportunities to do so."

Two things strike me as of special interest to architects in this argument. One is the implication that by taking over the job of "creating or enclosing" functionally organized space the industrial designer is not really doing anything that is of interest to architects. An architect's blood would, I should think, curdle at the word *merely* in the assertion that—so far as department stores and office buildings are concerned—the technique of creating or enclosing functional space is merely incidental. For if architecture is not that, what on earth is it?

The other thing worth noting is that there is not the slightest indication that the spokesman for the industrial designers wants to claim credit for them as architects. On the contrary, he is at pains to say explicitly that the industrial designer "does not claim to be an architectural specialist." (Notice that word *specialist*.) What he is proudly and clearly asserting is that industrial designers have a distinct and "unconventional" procedure, a "proved technique," with no resemblance to the procedures and techniques of architecture. If they are called upon to do jobs which people called architects used to do, that is just common sense, because the jobs are not those with which an "architectural specialist" would be concerned.

What, then, is the "proved" technique, the "unconventional" procedure, employed by the industrial designer? The answer, according to the annual, is that the technique is one of applying certain processes of analysis and synthesis. And this technique is then outlined in a paragraph which implies as much about the limitations of contemporary architects as it tells us directly about how an industrial designer works.

The paragraph opens with this sentence, in which that blood-curdling word *merely* crops up again: "Building design—which is merely a process of deciding how a given space shall be enclosed—is the last thing the industrial designer thinks of when he is asked to design a building." Without the slightest overtone of malice or aggressiveness, quite matter-of-factly, this sentence says that the sort of thing architects specialize in is entirely an external and superficial matter, of no immediate concern to an industrial designer faced with the job of designing a building. "Building design," in the context of the industrial designer's thought, is something you don't bother about until you have done the really important job, which is "to design a building."

The "unconventional procedure" which the industrial designer follows in designing a building such as a department store is then outlined thus:

> He first wants to know exactly what is to be done and accomplished in the space to be enclosed. . . . Here there is so much area to be allotted to each type of merchandise, and each must have certain special facilities and settings for storage, display, and selling; these departments have a logical relationship to each other, and while they become in effect a series of specialty shops, the transition from one to another must be easy, natural, comfortable. There are certain logical points at which customers will enter the premises; there is a desirable sequence in which the facilities of the store should be presented to the customer's attention; the customer's comfort and convenience must be considered at every point . . . a thousand details of operation must be provided for efficiently and unobtrusively.

Only after he has considered all these and innumerable other requirements, has discussed them with management, reconciled them with each other, and organized them in a satisfactory scheme, does the industrial designer "determine the structure that will enclose the whole." And even then, the annual tells us, he must be influenced by many "practical considerations," as opposed, one assumes, to aesthetic ones, such as the necessity for adequate identification (signs), for displays designed to attract the passer-by, for convenient and sheltered entrances and exits, for easy access to parking places, and so on. With the net result that his exterior design, when he gets to it, "grows naturally out of a balance of these requirements."

The Ideal Architect

What strikes me about this description of the industrial designer's "unconventional procedure" is its similarity to what was formerly thought to be the architect's function. Five centuries ago Leone Battista Alberti, the Florentine architect and architectural theorist, said that any common workman could "run up" a building "that is immediately necessary for any particular purpose, and about which there is no doubt of what sort it should be, or of the ability of the owner to afford it," but that "to raise an Edifice which is compleat in every part, and to consider and provide beforehand everything necessary for such a work" is the business of an architect.

"Him I call an Architect," Alberti said, "who . . . is able . . . to devise, and, with execution, to compleat all those works which . . . can . . . be adapted to the uses of mankind . . ." That (in Leoni's eighteenth-century translation) is the skeleton of the fifteenth-century humanist's definition of an architect. The essential elements of this definition are, I suppose, two: that it is the architect's job to devise and to complete the structure, and that the structures must be humanly useful.

I repeat, however, that this is only the skeleton of Alberti's definition. There are, in fact, five places where I have cut away from the basic structure of Alberti's thought those phrases by which he qualifies and extends its meaning. The full quotation reads as follows:

> Him I call an Architect, who, by a sure and wonderful Art and Method, is able, both with thought and invention, to devise, and, with execution, to compleat all those Works, which, by means of the movement of great Weights, and the conjunction and amassment of Bodies, can with the greatest Beauty, be adapted to the uses of Mankind: and to be able to do this, he must have a thorough insight into the noblest and most curious Sciences.

I quoted the grammatical skeleton, the basic framework of his conception, first by itself, without the subordinate qualifications and extensions, to emphasize the degree to which Alberti's conception of the architect subordinates the idea of Beauty to that of usefulness, and to call attention to the tremendous importance he attaches to a knowledge of the techniques of construction and planning. Notice that the architect's ability to "devise and compleat" his works is limited by three separate qualifications. First, he is able to do it only if he has the mastery of "a sure and wonderful" combination of art (by which Alberti means technique) and method. Even then he is not *able* unless he employs both thought and invention. (That word *invention*, of course, does not mean what we would call creative imagination; it is a technical term, in common use during the Renaissance to mean the disposition of the various conventional elements of a composition in new and appropriate arrangements.) Having interrupted himself twice to specify prerequisites to the architect's ability to "devise and compleat" his useful works, Alberti seems, for the moment, satisfied. But no sooner has he got to the end of his thought than he remembers still another reservation he wants to make. Art and method, thought and invention, are not, after all, enough to enable the architect to do his job. He must also have "a thorough insight into the noblest and most curious sciences." If he has all these things, he is able to build structures which can be adapted "with the greatest beauty" to the uses of mankind.

I do not want to underplay the significance Alberti attaches to "Beauty," about which he says a good deal in Book VI and Book IX of his treatise. "Beauty and ornament" (he likes to refer to them in tandem) are the sources of the "pleasure and delight" we take in looking at buildings. Beauty he defines as the harmony or congruity of all the parts of a structure; ornament he defines as something "added or fastened on" so that the unsightly parts of a structure will give less offense and the handsome parts will be even lovelier. (He therefore calls ornament a kind of "auxiliary brightness and improvement to Beauty.") In one place he even says that the architect's having satisfied necessity by his structure "is a very small matter," and that even if he has also achieved "conveniency" his building will give no pleasure if people are shocked by its "deformity." But when he returns to the subject later, he is careful to restore the balance. It should always be clear, he insists, that the architect has "consulted necessity and convenience in the first place."

First and foremost the architect is, in Alberti's phrase, the "Inventor of all Conveniences." Mankind, he tells us, is obligated to the architect not only for safe and pleasant shelters, but for having "contrived" many other things "of the highest use and convenience," such as sweat baths; aqueducts; tunnels; ships and vehicles; bridges; and engines of war. More victories in war, he says, have been won by the "art and skill" of the architects than by the conduct or fortune of the generals.

Versatility versus Specialization

The Renaissance flavor of all this, its undismayed recognition of the need for versatility, may well seem naïve to those of us who have been constantly reminded that ours is an age of specialization. We know (or at least we think we know) that a man who knows enough to build a bridge can't possibly know enough besides to design a church, let alone a sweat bath. Perhaps that is so; but it may be useful to entertain some doubts about it.

For myself, I wonder if our abject acceptance of compartmentalization and specialization is not in part the result of an understandable but disproportionate reverence for science. The sciences are, of course, highly specialized—so much so that it is almost impossible in an academic community to get the physicists and biologists and chemists and experimental psychologists to approve any joint offering, or even to endorse any course in the history of science. Their reluctance is soundly based in that it is quite literally impossible for any one person to know enough to be both a chemist and an experimental psychologist. The rise of such nominally overlapping sciences as bio-physics and bio-chemistry, far from being a sign of a unification of the sciences, is rather a sign of still greater specialization. A biologist or a physicist, I am told, could no more swap laboratories with a bio-physicist than a geologist could swap places with a botanist.

It is to specialization of this sort that we are indebted for much knowledge (or, more accurately, for vast quantities of relatively reliable data) about our world and ourselves. Architects know, as well as the rest of us, that the structures they design owe much to the data provided by highly specialized sciences. And by a peculiar distortion of logic they, like all of us, seem to conclude that, if specialization can produce such valuable data, it can do anything.

But of course it can't. It can produce data on the strength of materials, but it can't use the data. It can produce data on the psychological effects of texture and color, but it has no way of putting such data to use. As J. Robert Oppenheimer has bravely said, scientific knowledge, "by the very techniques, powers, and facts of its acquisition [which is to say, by its highly specialized procedures], precludes other knowledge." He points out that in a physics laboratory, for example, the kind of arrangement that is suitable for doing an experiment to find out *where* an atom is, precludes the possibility of acquiring knowledge about the rate at which it is moving. Not only does learning where a given atom is make it impossible to learn its velocity; it also, Oppenheimer tells us, "makes it logically contradictory to assume that the other quantity (i.e., velocity) has a value."

Scientific data can be acquired, in short, only by a system of rigid specialization. It is no wonder, therefore, that specialization has come to be honored and respected and—most important of all—enjoyed. The kind of knowledge which science can acquire—knowledge which is reliable to a relatively high degree—is, as Oppenheimer justly says, incredibly precious. And to the scientist the specialized procedure with which he acquires this knowledge—the process of acquiring it—understandably becomes an end in itself. "It is just the technique and the wonder of one's own ability to do it" that is for Oppenheimer "part of the value of it."

This delight in process is a characteristic feature of our American world. But scientific processes are not the only ones in which man may find delight, and neither the architect nor the physician nor the teacher nor the corporation executive nor the politician (nor the scientist, for that matter) need conclude that the only respectable or fruitful processes are those which, like the processes of science, are highly specialized. It is at least possible that, at this moment in history, the processes of synthesis and generalization may be even more fruitful than those of specialization.

By suggesting this possibility I do not wish to imply that I have any use for the notion, which even some very eminent scientists have flirted with, that there should be a moratorium on science. There cannot ever be too great a quantity of relatively reliable data available to mankind, though I am well aware that there may be too much for a given individual to cope with.

It does seem to me, however, that the individual's difficulty in coping with the flood of new data which has poured out of the scientists' laboratories is compounded by a mistaken sense that he has no right to the fruits of specialized techniques unless he has mastered the techniques by which they were produced. We tell one another, in dozens of ways, that this is so. In an agony of self-depreciation we tell ourselves that we should be ashamed if we drive cars whose inner functioning we do not understand, or if we listen to music emitted by a device whose electronic complexities are beyond us. In part this sense of guilt is the result of the scientists' own insistence that the popularization (or making generally available) of the results of their highly specialized techniques is naughty and disreputable, and in part it is simply the result of a vestigial puritanism which makes us feel guilty about having anything which we didn't earn by the sweat of our bodies or minds. As if life itself were not a gift.

There are, of course, very good reasons why all of us, including architects, should be aware of the distinction between firsthand and secondhand knowledge. But there are also very good reasons why we should not try to require of ourselves a firsthand knowledge of all the data upon which we form our judgments and decisions. Which is simply another way of saying that we must all be (as in fact we all are) generalists as well as specialists. There are also good reasons why, in these days, some of us should specialize in being generalists. Which is another way of saying we need architects, in Alberti's sense of the term, as well as poets and philosophers.

The Heart as Nucleus

Thanks, in part at least, to the idea of specialization, the procedures which to Alberti seemed to distinguish an architect from a common workman now seem, to the industrial designers, to distinguish them from architects. If the industrial designers are correct, it is no wonder that they are being asked to undertake jobs which architects would formerly have been expected to do. Nor is it surprising that Buckminster Fuller, who has designed some of the most creative and elegant structures of this century, should emphatically insist that he is not an architect but "a research department for architecture." One is reminded of the "thorough insight into the noblest and most curious sciences" which Alberti's architect had to have.

I have discussed these matters with friends who are architects, but they do not seem to be alarmed by having lost to industrial designers a few commissions for stores, chains of service stations, and airliners. They have plenty to do anyway, and if they have any uneasiness about what is happening they cover it by slightly disdainful references to the industrial designers' penchant for publicity. With all respect for the professional honor of the architects I happen to know, I have never noticed that architects in general are unduly hampered by professional ethics in calling attention to themselves and their talents. One has heard of Frank Lloyd Wright and Mies van der Rohe.

But one has also heard that Mies's roofs leak, and that in the kitchen of Wright's masterpiece, the Imperial Hotel, things were so designed that there was no way to get at and clean up the bug-heaven of food and grease which accumulated behind the ill-placed stoves. Small matters, these, when set against the visual delight which Mies and Wright have created by "building design." But if I were footing the bill for a new apartment house or hotel, not to say a gas station or airliner, I would probably turn, however regretfully, to a designer who thought *first* about the "comfort and convenience" of the people who would use it, and about providing "efficiently and unobtrusively" for the thousand and one details of the operations (including living) which would be carried out in it.

Nor would I assume, in making my choice, that I was thereby running a great risk of getting a structure which, though efficient and convenient, was likely to be deformed and unsightly. I remember Thoreau's observation that whatever architectural beauty he saw about him had "gradually grown from within outward, out of the necessities and character of the indweller . . . without ever a thought for the appearance"—and when I remember it, I do not think it is perverse or romantic nonsense. It reminds me in turn of Horatio Greenough's admonition to American architects over a century ago: "Instead of forcing the functions of every sort of building into one general form, adopting an outward shape for the sake of the eye or of association," let us, he said, "begin from the heart as a nucleus, and work outward." I take the word *heart*, in this passage, in both its senses.

Ballerinas in Polo Coats

To the extent that the architect combines in his own person the builder and the engineer as well as the artist, to the extent, in other words, that he exemplifies Alberti's ideal and has avoided the illusion that the specialization essential to science is also desirable in the arts—to that extent he will be directly responsive to the life about him. But the architect as specialist, as designer pure and simple, seems to be primarily responsive not to life but to architecture.

The idea that artists may be more responsive to art than to life was first suggested to me by a remark made by a very great teacher when I was in graduate school. The teacher was Mark Van Doren, lecturing on epic poetry. He had the great teacher's gift of saying things parenthetically, in the midst of something else he was saying, which did not interrupt the main thread of his discourse but which later grew and developed in fascinating profusion—as if the enclosing parenthesis formed a sort of pot in which the planted idea could germinate while the lecture went on, and in which you could take it away afterward, if you wanted to, and watch it grow.

What he said parenthetically on this occasion was, if I remember correctly: "Of course poetry is not inspired by life, but by other poetry. It is not the girl you are in love with who inspires you to write a sonnet, but some sonnet you have read about some other girl." I remember being horrified by the remark because I had just written a sonnet about a girl and wanted very much to believe it was a direct response to her charms. Some years later, however, I came upon that sonnet and ruefully discovered no trace of the flesh and blood girl in it though there were some painfully evident traces of one of the limper sonnets of John Keats.

To a considerable extent what Mark Van Doren said is true not only of poetry but of all the arts. Each of us, of course, instinctively seeks to arrange the elements of his environment in satisfying patterns of color, sound, texture, and so on, and a human being who was cut off from acquaintance with traditions of art would promptly set about improvising patterns and forms of his own. But in a society where we are surrounded by paintings, music, poems, and architecture it is impossible to respond to the unadorned reality about us with senses unaffected (or should I say untrained) by our predecessor's selectively ordered reflections of it. It is probably not a landscape, but a painting of a landscape, which drives the incipient painter to canvas and brush. So too the incipient architect is probably inspired less by the physical, social, and cultural realities of his environment than by the work of his fellow architects, living and dead.

Van Doren's comment raises, of course, the question of how, if art is initially inspired by art rather than by life, art ever got started. Obviously someone must at some point have produced a painting in direct response to a human figure or a natural landscape, because at some point there can have been no other paintings to prompt him. There must have been a first house, a first temple, a first pyramid, designed (or improvised, if you prefer—though the terms are more nearly synonymous than we usually admit) as a direct response to physical factors and to such basic social needs as those for shelter, for worship, or for the assurance of immortality. The forms which have been developed and refined, echoed and re-echoed in our various traditions of design, obviously had their origins in primordial responses to physical and social realities, unhelped and unhindered by earlier formal solutions.

Once a formal solution has been found, of course, it tends to be repeated; and the better the solution is, the more it will affect subsequent buildings. In architecture, as in the other arts, it is with forms developed over a long period by many craftsmen that the creative artist works. It is these traditional forms which provide him with the vehicle for his perceptions. They serve him as the conventions of ballet serve the dancer, and become in effect the conventional costume he puts on while dancing his own dance. A ballerina wearing the standard frilled *tutu* and moving in a traditional *pas de deux* is a good deal freer to express her unique vision than one wearing a polo coat.

I am sure there must be an architectural equivalent to what Robert Frost said about the exigencies of traditional verse forms. As Frost put it, writing poetry without rhyme or meter is like playing tennis with the net down.

Frost's remark is especially useful in our context because it permits us to ask whether there are not other nets than traditional English rhyme and meter which may put zest into the game of poetry. And of course, a number of poets, including such diverse figures as Walt Whitman, greatest of American poets, and the Japanese haiku writers from Matsuo Bashō to Masaoka Shiki, played the game with nets very unlike the traditional net of English verse and very unlike each other's.

There are those who would argue that it is one thing for a Japanese poet, who belongs after all to a different culture, to use a net unlike the one we are used to, but quite another thing for Whitman (and his successors) to do so. Whitman seems to them, as it were, a traitor to his class, willfully seeking a flatulent originality. The literary argument roughly parallels the architectural one which has been employed in Henry Hope Reed, Jr.'s, recent book denouncing modern architecture in all its manifestations, on the ground that it has merely seceded from tradition in a fruitless effort to be original. The author passionately recommends instead a new courthouse for San Francisco in what is called "the high classical manner," with "rusticated arched entrances, marked keystones, gold lanterns, and statues in profusion," all designed by a man identified as (and I quote) "an interested amateur who resides in Berkeley, across the bay."

In a sense the argument is sound. If we assume that the American world we live in is the same world whose "life" originally inspired the forms which were refined and developed by the great artists of the past, there is indeed no excuse for an urgent search for new or significant forms. The artist will employ the forms indigenous to his culture, as Milton and Wordsworth employed the sonnet form, not fretting at their "narrow gloom" but rejoicing in the knowledge that he has at his command vehicles relevant to the experience of his fellow men, in which he can express his own personal vision of life's abiding charm, or wonder, or horror (for all three, I am afraid, abide). As long as there is a basic continuity in the culture, the traditional forms retain a valid relation to the vital forces in contemporary life. Modifications will, of course, be necessary as time brings gradual change. But there is no danger that artistic conservatism will resist them effectively. Society has plenty of built-in devices to induce even the most recalcitrant architect to adapt his work in some measure to contemporary reality—one of the most effective, the client's bank roll.

But what if the world we live in is not a mere evolutionary modification of the culture which dominated the Western world a thousand years ago? What if the world we still sometimes think we are living in has been so transfigured by unprecedented influences that it is in effect a new ethnical epoch? What if technology and science really have made fundamental changes in man's relation to the natural world about him, to his fellow men, and to God?

There have been times during the past century or so when people talked as if technology and science *had* produced such fundamental changes. But it is characteristic of the persistence of our mental and emotional habits that people in general have not acted as if they believed it, and have generally refused to listen if anyone spoke bluntly about the consequences. At the turn of the century, for example, the American engineer and bridge builder, George S. Morison, wrote a moving and impressive book arguing that the discovery of ways to manufacture power had initiated changes which during the next couple of centuries would be more far-reaching than any brought about by earlier epochal advances such as the use of fire, the domestication of animals, or the invention of written alphabets. Writing in 1898, Morison foresaw that the new technology would bring almost inconceivable changes not only in material ways but in man's social and intellectual life. Let me quote a brief passage:

> The manufacture of power . . . has separated power from the mind which must manage it; it calls for intelligent design and direction of the multitude of works which it has rendered possible; it has equipped our generation with tools for study and investigation as well as for mechanical work. The new epoch will alter the relations between the professions, business, and trades; it will readjust the duties of government and the relations of one government to another; it will change our system of education.
> . . . The new epoch differs from all preceding epochs, in that while they represented successive periods of progress, different races existed simultaneously in every period of advancement, whereas the new epoch must from its very nature soon become universal . . . It brings all races together, and must in time remove all differences in capacity.

This quoted passage deals in generalizations; but Morison's book is specific. Referring to architecture, for example, he notes that the manufacture of power "has made the demands of the new epoch so different from those of the old that nearly everything which has to be used must be built anew." In the new epoch, he said, "architecture, which as a fine art would consign itself to the museum, and which sometimes, following the rapid changes of fashion, seems to differ from millinery chiefly in the want of a beautiful object on which to place its novelties, will find its highest development in correct construction."

One would have thought that in the days when the Bauhaus influence was in its ascendancy, architectural theorists would have rediscovered Morison's book, and perhaps even given some attention to the house he designed and built in Peterboro, New Hampshire. But they did not, and I suspect that the reason is that he was too blunt in his insistence that the new epoch is really new. We all talk wistfully at times about "a new heaven and a new earth," and to generations of men "the new world" has seemed, at moments at least, to be a social and cultural possibility as well as a geographical reality. But the new is unfamiliar, and unfamiliarity as well as familiarity breeds contempt. When we move into our new glass box we are likely to take grandmother's rocker and somebody else's grandfather's cobbler's bench along with us.

I suppose that our basic dislike and distrust of the new epoch and the emergent forms appropriate to it is the result of two facts: first, that as Morison foresaw, it has opened as an era of destruction. He understood that the new epoch would "from its very nature destroy many of the conditions which give most interest to the history of the past, and many of the traditions which people hold most dear." Looking back from our moment in time, we can see that he was right in prophesying that there would be, for perhaps a century or more, "great destruction of old buildings, old boundaries, and old monuments, and furthermore of customs and ideas, systems of thought and methods of education." And destruction is sad—so sad that, like death, it sometimes appears to us to be tragic.

The destruction has come, and will continue, not, Morison said, because the things which are destroyed are in themselves bad, but "because however good and useful they may have been in the past, they are not adapted to fulfill the requirements of the new epoch." The danger is that the destructive changes will come so fast that the new developments, appropriate to the new world, do not come fast enough to fill the gap between them. And of course such developments (in architecture, education, or whatever) will not come fast enough if, each time we are frightened by some destructive change, we decide that change itself is bad and that we must therefore renounce all attempts at new solutions and go back, as the phrase is, to "the high classical manner," or the theology of Aquinas, or the politics of Aristotle, or whatever the "unchanging verity" in our neck of the woods may be.

The Wellsprings of Design

It is my conviction that the society we live in marks—as Morison said it did—a really new epoch, but that it is shaped not by technology and science alone but by a unique combination of forces, a compound of scientific technology and the spirit of democracy. Some years ago—more than a decade—I tried to suggest that these twin forces had been revolutionizing man's conception of his relations to nature, his fellow man, and his gods, for more than a century, and that the elements of the emergent environment produced by these twin forces were for many years shaped not by our artists but by untutored citizens working without any "artistic" pretensions. It is the patterns and forms these people evolved which the artists of our time must arrange (and have begun to arrange) in patterns and forms satisfactorily expressing the values and attitudes appropriate to the new epoch.

It was my contention that the early, unschooled attempts to create satisfying patterns out of these novel elements in our environment constituted a new kind of folk art. The folk arts we are familiar with are the product of groups cut off from the main stream of contemporary life, and they are the surviving remnants of traditional forms and patterns. These new "folk arts" are, on the contrary, the product of people directly involved with the dynamic forces of contemporary life, and their forms and patterns have no precedent, since the environmental elements to which they give shape are quite literally something new.

In order to distinguish them from the more familiar folk arts, I labeled these the vernacular arts—meaning by that the empirical attempts of ordinary people to shape the elements of their everyday environment in a democratic, technological age. Specifically, I meant the books, buildings, and artifacts of all sorts whose forms have been shaped as a direct response to the new elements which democracy and technology have introduced into our environment within the past hundred and fifty years.

The buildings produced in such a vernacular tradition (as, for example, the early balloon-frame houses of the American Midwest) were often ugly. So it is easy for the admirers of the "high classical" manner in courthouses to dismiss them as "mere inventions in the construction industry" and to accuse those of us who are interested in them of writing the kind of architectural discussion which would consider Venetian architecture solely in terms of pile-driving. But this misses the point.

The point about the balloon-frame houses which came out of Chicago in the 1830's and spread all across America in the following decades, is that their builders empirically discovered a form which took full advantage of machine-made lumber and machine-made nails and machine transportation (three elements of the technological environment which traditional architecture had no use for), and a form, furthermore, which also incorporated the elements of economy, speed of construction, mobility, flexibility, and universal availability fostered by the spirit of democracy. And, finally, the point is that out of this anonymous, unrefined form, later architects evolved structures which, by any valid standards, are architecture of a very high order indeed, however unrelated they may be to the more massive and rigid architecture of hand-hewn beams and hand-hewn stone, incorporating the aristocratic and hierarchical values of order and stability.

We could illustrate the role of the vernacular in evolving new forms, appropriate to the new environment, by reference to other examples, including the steel frame and the concrete shell. But the point would be the same: that in a time of rapid and future-founding change, the architect who ignores the vernacular, with its unself-conscious and uninhibited response to the elements of a new environment, and who submits himself too devoutly to the inspiration of past architecture (his own, or that of others) runs a grave risk of losing fruitful contact with the life about him.

The risk is compounded, I think, in our time by the degree to which criticism of the arts is replacing the arts themselves as the source of artistic inspiration. I know that in the literary arts this is so, and I have the impression that just as there is a good deal of poetry which owes more to the critics than to

133

other poetry (let alone to life), so there is a good deal of architecture these days which owes more to what the writers in architectural magazines say than it does to aesthetic realities. It would be a pity, I think, if we were to have a plague of architects who are less excited by architecture than by writers who are excited about architecture.

But if architects should, as Mark Van Doren's comment implied, properly take their inspiration from architecture, it seems important in these rapidly changing times that they include under that head not only the masterpieces of the past but, more especially, the inchoate vernacular which is still springing up around them in direct response to the new elements democracy and technology are continuously introducing into the lives of people everywhere. Architectural criticism generally admires architecture that is cognate with the achievements of the great artists of the recent and remoter past. But great artists never imitate their equals; they plagiarize from their inferiors.

Architects who submit to the influence of architectural critics will be hounded into the shadow of some imperious, though dead, perfection. But the perfection embodied in the great architecture of the past, as in the great poetry and great painting, was the culmination of a growth which began far back in the inexpert gropings of ordinary mortals. The forms which reached their loveliest and most moving expression in the Gothic cathedrals of the Middle

Ages were evolved not from those of classical temples but from those of common barns and markets, just as Beethoven's symphonies were an elaboration of formal elements originating in folk music, and just as Shakespeare's plays were the culmination of a long development in the popular theater. We tend to forget that Shakespeare did not write *King Lear* because he was steeped in Aeschylus and Sophocles, but because he found in the crude forms evolved by generations of inferior predecessors a vehicle, relevant to his time, which he could adapt and refine so that it fitly conveyed a vision of life which his genius made relevant to all times.

Vernacular forms, whose elements are the materials and processes of technology and the attitudes and interests of democracy, will continue to be improvised wherever technology and democracy make themselves felt among the peoples of the earth. They will, of course, be modified in each region by physical and social actualities and by the local cultural heritage which becomes part of the fabric of what we build. But they will share the quality of immediate responsiveness to the driving energies of the new epoch. They will be crude, unrefined, and—if you will—ugly, more often than not. But they are the most life-giving of all the wellsprings of design, and if the architect indeed vanishes from the contemporary scene it will be because he mistook them for less.

What Is "American" in Architecture and Design?*

NOTES TOWARD AN AESTHETIC OF PROCESS

* This essay is a revised and expanded version of an article published originally in *Art in America*, Fall 1958.

ALL OF US AT TIMES need to confirm the continuity of our culture with that of the past, in order to reassure ourselves in the midst of bewildering flux and change. The author of the so-called "uncertainty principle" in modern physics, Nobel prize-winner Werner Heisenberg, has himself felt such a need, and recently went to some length to "prove" that he owes his eminence in atomic physics to an early reading of Plato's *Timaeus* and a sound training in the Greek natural philosophers.

We may ask what is "American" in architecture and design because we want to establish their continuity with buildings and objects of the past. And if this is our motive in asking the question we will, of course, be most interested in those buildings and objects whose structure and aesthetic effect are clearly related to, and thus comparable with, those of their predecessors in the Western tradition. We will concern ourselves, that is, with architecture in its textbook sense, as a fine art which has developed continuously, with local and national variants, throughout the Western world.

If we approach the question in this way, taking "architecture" to mean churches, government buildings, and palaces (for princes or merchants), and taking "design" to include what the nineteenth century lumped as "Industrial Art" (manufactured objects to which one could apply "arts and crafts" decoration, such as pottery, textiles, bijouterie, and the printed page), we will probably conclude that the "American" quality is catholicity. We can find in the United States an imitation of almost any architectural style or decorative mannerism which ever existed in any other nation. And when we have done so, all we shall have demonstrated is what we already knew: that Americans came from everywhere, and brought with them the traditions—architectural and decorative as well as social and religious—of which they were the heirs. We shall have learned what is English or Spanish or German about our architecture and our design, and therefore how they relate to the Western tradition; but we shall know as little as ever about their "American" quality, if such there be.

There is, for example, nothing "American" about New York City's Cathedral of St. John the Divine, except perhaps the fact that it is unfinished. It is an important and lovely fact of our cultural history and of the history of architecture in this country, but it tells us more about what is not "American" than about what is, just as a Coca-Cola bottle made in

France tells us more about what is "American" than about what is French.

The question can be asked, however, not in hopes of establishing ties to the past but in hopes of discovering those elements of creative energy and vitality which can evolve forms and structures appropriate to a world of flux and change—the "American" world—even at the risk of devaluing or destroying much that we have cherished and loved in the past. If this is our motive, we must look at those structures and objects which were not thought of as "Architecture" or "Industrial Art" by those who designed or paid for them. We must look, in other words, at those structures and objects which have been unselfconsciously evolved from the new materials, and for the unprecedented psychological and social uses present in the "American" environment.

The Vitality of the Vernacular

If we go at the question in this way, we will discover, I think, that the "American" quality is the product of a vernacular which has flourished in the United States but is by no means confined to it, which has deep roots in Western Europe, and which is rapidly establishing itself wherever modern technology and democracy are working together to recast our consciousness of our relations to one another, to external nature, and to our Gods.

I am again using the term *vernacular* as a de-

Above, Robertson's Milling Machine, Patented 1852 (from a wood engraving in an advertisement in David Bigelow, *History of Prominent Mercantile and Manufacturing Firms in the United States*, Boston, 1857); *upper right*, A Brainerd Universal Milling Machine of 1894 (from a wood engraving in *Illustrated Price List* of the Fairbanks Co., 1894); and, *lower right*, the Cincinnati Milling Machine Company's Universal Milling Machine of 1943 (from the *American Machinist*, May 27, 1943).

scriptive label for the patterns and forms which people have devised, usually anonymously, in attempting to give satisfying order to the unprecedented
elements which democracy and technology have
jointly introduced into the human environment during
the past hundred and fifty years or so.

Actually there are two ways in which people
can order the elements of a new environment. One
is to cramp them into patterns or forms which were
originally devised to order other and quite different
elements of another and quite different environment.
Hence the mid-nineteenth-century blank verse
"epics" about backwoodsmen in Kentucky; hence the
flying buttresses of Raymond Hood's Chicago Tribune Tower; hence "symphonic" jazz and amphora-
shaped cigarette lighters. The forms or patterns in
such instances will often have a symmetry and finish
which give genuine (if nostalgic) pleasure, but only
at the cost of considerable distortion of the elements
which have been worried into them. It would be interesting to consider, for example, how we warped
the development of a system of higher education appropriate to an "American" world by corseting it in
pseudo-medieval cloisters and pseudo-Renaissance
palaces.

The other way is to shuffle and rearrange the
unfamiliar elements until some appropriate design is
empirically discovered. The vernacular patterns or
forms so devised will often be ungainly, crude, or
awkward in contrast with those evolved and refined

over the centuries to order the elements of the pre-democratic, pre-industrial world, but they will at least bear a vital relation to the new environment of whose elements they are composed. More importantly, they will contain within themselves the potentiality of refinement and—God willing—of transfiguration by the hand of genius.

As an example of the characteristic evolution of vernacular form, we may take the development of a machine tool such as the milling machine. Three stages in its design are illustrated. The earliest machine shown in the series was made forty years after Eli Whitney created his first practical machine tool of this type, but it is still a gawky four-legged object which has not yet discovered the so-called "knee and column" form appropriate to its functions, in which both of the later machines are made. Bearing in mind that each stage in the development of this machine represents an advance in the magnitude and complexity of the operations it is designed to perform, even a non-mechanic will be able to observe the increasing simplicity and refinement of the over-all design.

If we turn from mechanics to building we may perhaps more easily see the way in which vernacular forms and patterns can become expressive elements in creative design. In the past thirty years many structural elements which were developed in vernacular building have become characteristic features of contemporary architecture. One has only to look

Left, Cast Iron Building designed and built by James Bogardus, 1848, on northwest corner of Washington and Murray streets, New York (photograph courtesy Gottscho-Schleisner; *below left,* The Hotel del Coronado, on San Diego Bay, California, 1889 (wood engraving from promotional pamphlet, *Coronado Beach,* Oakland, 1890); *below,* Abandoned Tobacco Factory in Louisville, Kentucky (photograph 1943, courtesy of Reynolds Metal Co., which bought the building that year for conversion to aircraft-parts manufacture).

at the accompanying pictures of a century-old iron loft building, the glass-enclosed verandahs of a seaside hotel of the eighteen eighties, and an abandoned tobacco factory to be aware of the vernacular roots of important elements in the architectural design of such buildings as Albert Kahn's tank arsenal, the Farm Security Administration's utility building for a California migrant camp, and Raymond Hood's magnificent McGraw-Hill building—done after he had learned to dispense with the Gothic trappings of the Tribune Tower.

Chrysler Tank Arsenal,
[desig]ned by Albert Kahn, 1940
[Hedr]ich-Blessing Studio, cour-
[tesy] of *Architectural Forum*);
[abov]e, Utilities Building, FSA
[Camp], Woodville, California
[photo]graph courtesy Library
[of C]ongress); *right,* The
[McGr]aw-Hill Building, West
[Forty-]second Street, New York,
[desig]ned by Raymond Hood,
[1931] (photograph courtesy
[McGr]aw-Hill Studio).

Thus far we have touched upon examples of the vernacular which were evolved primarily to cope with or exploit those elements of the new environment which were introduced by technology—by developments in the machining of metal, in frame construction, and in the manufacture of glass. But the vernacular as I have tried to define it is by no means the product of technology alone. It is a response to the simultaneous impact of technology and democracy. Watt's first practical steam engine and the Declaration of Independence became operative in the same year, we should remember. Technology by itself can become the servant of a tyrant, as has been amply proved in Hitler's Germany and Stalin's Russia and, on a smaller scale, in some communities closer to home. But it is the peculiar blend of technology with democracy which produces vernacular as opposed to merely technological forms. New technics and new materials have not been the only constituents of the new environment for which men have had to discover appropriate forms. There have also been new amalgams of thought, of emotion, and of attitude.

If, for a moment, I may use the term "American" in its conventional and limited sense, as referring to whatever has to do with the United States, it is a very American fact that we are chiefly indebted to a European for calling our attention to the anonymous and "undignified" sources of many of the creative elements in contemporary architecture and design. It

was the Swiss scholar Siegfried Giedion, who, in the
Norton lectures at Harvard in 1939, first showed
many of us that such utilitarian structures as the
balloon-frame houses of early Chicago, and such
utilitarian objects as nineteenth-century water pails
and railway seats, were often more prophetic of the
essential spirit and creative force of our contemporary arts than the buildings and objects which have
been acclaimed for their "artistic" quality.

By now it is clear that many of the constituents
of contemporary design which at first struck us as
alien and strange evolved from our vernacular. The
molded plywood which seemed so startling when it
appeared in chairs exhibited at the Museum of
Modern Art in the late thirties and early forties was
the conventional material for seats in American
ferryboats in the 1870's. The spring-steel cantilever
principle, which attracted world-wide attention when
Mies van der Rohe used it in a chair he designed at
the Bauhaus, had been standard in the seats of
American reapers and mowers and other farm machines since the 1850's. Built-in furniture, the "storage wall," and movable partitions to create flexible
interior space, all three were employed in an ingenious amateur house plan worked out in the 1860's
by Harriet Beecher Stowe's sister, Catherine Beecher,
a pioneer in the field now known as home economics.
The provision of storage facilities in interchangeable
units, which can be rearranged or added to, as changing needs and circumstances require, had a long

history in office equipment, kitchen cabinets, and sectional furniture before it was recognized as an appropriate element in creative design.

What is important about such instances, from the point of view of this article, is that so many of them reflect a concern with process, especially as it is manifest in motion and change; for it is this concern, as I have said, which seems to me to be central to that "American" quality which we are trying to define.

The Syntax of Momentum

Wherever we look in the field of the vernacular we will discover such designs. Let us look, for example, at a column of text from the first guidebook published for travelers on the transcontinental railroad, reproduced at right. No one, I suppose, would select such a page for inclusion in an exhibit of graphic arts; but if we examine it attentively we will discover many elements of typography and layout which tell us more about the dynamics of our civilization than any page we are likely to find included in the "Fifty Best Books of the Year" or any similar exhibit.

The general structure of the book from which it is taken (the *Great Trans-Continental Tourist's Guide . . . over the Union Pacific Railroad, Central Pacific Railroad . . .* , New York, 1870) is dictated, of course, by the westward journey. The main line schools and churches are in a flourishing condition. The United States Branch Mint of Nevada is located at this place. The newspaper interest is represented by the Carson *Appeal*, a daily paper, which has long been established here.

Carson City is situated in the center of the best farming land on Carson river, and the best in this part of the State. Carson is connected by stage with Genoa, Markleville and Silver Mountain. A narrow-gauge railroad has been built from Carson to Virginia City, which will be pushed forward to a connection with the Central Pacific at an early day.

GENOA CITY,

Fourteen miles southwest from Carson, is a thriving town of about 500 inhabitants, situated in a fine section of farming country on the Carson river, on the stage road to

MARKLEVILLE,

A mining town, in the State of California, on the eastern slope of the Sierras, containing about 600 inhabitants.

SILVER MOUNTAIN,

Another mining town, 14 miles from Silver Mountain, containing about 400 inhabitants. The country abounds in silver mines around these towns.

Leaving the mines and Carson City, we once more return to Reno and resume our journey west. Near by Reno the hills are loftier, nearer the river, and covered with pine forests, and as we enter the canyon we seem to have entered a cooler, pleasanter, and more invigorating atmosphere. The aroma of the spruce and pine is pleasant when compared with that of the alkaline plains. It is related of an Eastern lumberman, from "away down in Maine," who had been very sour and taciturn during the trip across the plains, refusing to be sociable with any of his fellow travelers, that when he entered within the shades of the forest, he straightened himself up in the cars for a moment, looked around, and exclaiming, "Thank God, I smell pitch once more," sank back in his seat and wept for joy.

Among these hills, with the river rolling along on our right, we pass along merrily, the dry, barren desert, forgotten in the new scenes opening to our view, until we reach

VERDI,

A station 11 miles west from Reno. Elevation, 4,915 feet. On, up the river, with its foaming current, now on our left, first on one side, then on the other, runs this beautiful stream, until we lose sight of it altogether. The road crosses and re-crosses it on fine Howe truss bridges, running as straight as the course of the mountains will permit. The mountains tower up on either hand, in places, sloping and covered with timber from base to summit, in others, precipitous, and covered with masses of black, broken rock. 'Tis a rough country, the canyon of the Truckee, possessing many grand and imposing features. Occasional strips of meadow land are seen, close to the river's edge, but too small and rocky to be of use, only as grazing land. Now, we cross the dividing line, and shout

as we enter California, a few miles east of

BOCA,

A station, 16 miles west of Verdi. Elevation, 5,560 feet. The lumber interest is well represented here, huge piles of ties, boards and timber lining the roadside. The river seems to be the means of transportation for the saw logs, immense numbers of them being scattered up and down the stream, with here and

---

Facsimile of page 154 in the *Great Trans-Continental Tourist's Guide*, New York, 1870, the first guidebook published for passengers on the recently completed transcontinental railroad.

of narrative and description follows the moving train past towns, settlements, and natural features along the route, with digressive loops to include sidetracks and feeder lines—both stagecoaches and railroads. To help the reader keep track of where he is, and to make it easy to find the portions of the text dealing with particular localities or topics, the author—or typesetter—broke the type columns into sections, with subheads in capital letters. Early in the book these subheads are merely phrases which serve the familiar function of titles for sections dealing with such matters as THE FAR WEST, ROLLING STOCK, and LAND GRANT. But at the point where the actual journey by train begins, something happens to these subheads, typographically and syntactically, which has a good deal to do with the jazz-like sensation of momentum which the book produces. The change occurs near the end of the "chapter" of the text which is headed OMAHA. The general description of this town, which was the starting point for the trip on the new transcontinental railroad, is subdivided into various sections, each of which deals with some important aspect of the town. The last of these is headed OMAHA BARRACKS. Typographically it appears to be a section consisting of three paragraphs, followed by another section dealing with SUMMIT LANDING (A FLAG STATION); but that's not what really happens.

Paragraph three begins as if it were going to be, like its two predecessors, about the barracks. The

first sentence reads: "At present there is no chaplain."
But that is the only sentence about the barracks. The
next one, in spite of a conjunction which looks as if
it tied what follows tightly to the idea that there
was no chaplain at the barracks, gets us on board
the train and on our way:

> But we must take our leave of Omaha, as
> the whistle is sounding its warning signal
> to step into the cars and commence our
> journey over the plains to the far west.
> We pass along through the suburbs of the
> town for about four miles, when we arrive
> at

> **SUMMIT LANDING**
> **(A FLAG STATION.)**

> at an altitude of 1142 feet. We are leaving
> the busy hum . . .

What has happened here is that the typography
(like the syntax) has been overridden by the impe-
tus of the narrative. And from this point on, with
only occasional relapses into conventional treatment,
the subheads are not permitted to halt or slow the
westward momentum.

The designer of the layout—whether this was
the author or the typesetter—obviously does not
know, however, quite how to cope with this new
form which he has contrived—or which his material
has forced upon him. Sometimes he puts a period

at the end of the subhead, even though the words in it are grammatically a part of what follows; at other times he uses a comma.

> Eleven miles further we arrive at
>
> ### COLTON.
>
> A new station six miles east of
>
> ### SIDNEY,
>
> Nebraska Territory. Company F, of the ninth infantry is stationed here. . . .

Sometimes he uses a small letter, sometimes an uncalled-for capital letter, to begin the new typographical section; at other times he both indents and capitalizes the first word, even though there is no grammatical break whatever.

At first the subheads which are incorporated into this run-on pattern are the names of towns or settlements through which the train passes. After a while, however, the pattern becomes habitual and is extended to all sorts of topics and subtopics. And by the time we cross the boundary into California— in that part of the text reproduced here—an illustration, the seal of the state, is incorporated into the momentum of the narrative syntax. Crude as it is, this pattern of picture-text continuity, contrived almost seventy years ago, is more "advanced" than anything we are likely to find in this week's slickest picture magazine. The anonymous designer who

stumbled upon it was no William Morris, either in
his respect for craftsmanship or in his mistrust of
the world which technology and democracy were
collaborating to create. One may doubt that his
knowledge of Greek philosophy and science went
much beyond the Archimedean exclamation in the
California seal, but the "American" world whose
values and attitudes he shared, and for some of
whose elements he improvised a suitable pattern,
was one to which a world-view like that of mid-
twentieth-century physics would not seem alien. It
was a world which seems, in retrospect, to have
been at least subconsciously aware that, as Werner
Heisenberg said in a recent lecture on *Quantum
Theory and the Roots of Atomic Science*, energy is
the substance from which all things are made; that
"energy is in fact that which moves; it may be
called the primary cause of all change."

The Aesthetics of Process

In an earlier essay I have tried to show that
the quality shared by all those things which are
recognized, here and abroad, as distinctively "American"—from skyscrapers to jazz to chewing gum—is
an awareness of, if not a delight in, process: that
universal "process of development" which, as Lancelot Law Whyte has said, man shares with all
organic nature, and which forever debars him from
achieving the perfection and eternal harmony of

which the great arts of Western Europe have for centuries created the illusion. In the hierarchical civilizations of the past, where systems of status kept people as well as values pretty much in their places, men were insulated against an awareness of process to an extent which is no longer possible. In an environment dominated by technology and democracy, a world of social and physical mobility and rapid change, we cannot escape it. And our awareness of process is inevitably reflected in the vernacular, just as our occasional dread of it is witnessed by our continuing commitment to the cultivated forms inherited from a world in which permanence and perfection seemed, at least, to be realities.

It is the ideas, emotions, and attitudes generated by this conscious or unconscious awareness of process which account, I think, for a basic difference between the aesthetic effects of vernacular forms and those of the cultivated Western tradition. Inevitably, the forms appropriate to our contemporary world lack the balanced symmetry, the stability, and the elaborate formality to which we are accustomed in the architecture and design of the past. They tend, instead, to be resilient, adaptable, simple, and unceremonious. Serenity gives way to tension. Instead of an aesthetic of the arrangement of mass, we have an aesthetic of the transformation of energy. Only in some such terms as these, it seems to me, can we describe the so-called "American" quality which we detect in our architecture and design.

It is not possible in a brief essay to do more than suggest the implications of such an approach to the question asked in our title. Obviously it restricts our attention to a limited field of structures and objects, and diverts it from some of the most charming and interesting things which have been produced in this country. But it has the merit, I think, of converting a question which can easily become a mere excuse for a naïvely nationalist antiquarianism, or an equally naïve internationalism, into one which may help us discover the aesthetic resources of an "open-ended" civilization, of an "American" environment which reaches far beyond the borders of the United States. It also has the modest merit of requiring us to look with fresh eyes at things around us—not just the things in the decorators' shops and museums, but the humbler things which, because the people who made them took them, as we do, for granted, are often spontaneously expressive of those elements in our environment which do not fall naturally into traditional forms and patterns.

One way to emphasize the point I am trying to make is to contrast a product of the vernacular with a masterpiece of the cultivated tradition. Books on the architecture of bridges do not, so far as I know, refer to structures such as the bridge built in 1882 across the Canyon Diablo in Arizona, on what is now the Santa Fe Railroad. Seen in contrast with the majestic Pont du Gard, one of the most perfect examples of Roman masonry construction, which rises 155 feet above the river Gard near the French city of Nîmes, this spider-web truss of iron, carrying heavy locomotives and cars 222 feet above the bottom of the canyon, dramatically illustrates the utterly different aesthetic effects produced in response not only to new technics and materials but also to new attitudes and values. The two structures, embodying fundamentally different conceptions of time, of space, of motion, and of man's relation to external nature, make essentially different demands upon our attention.

If we can put aside, for the time being, all question of which structure is the more beautiful, there will be no difficulty in recognizing which of the two is embodied in a scheme of forms that is capable of becoming a vehicle for an architecture expressive of the American environment.

In the triumphant composure of its daring triple arcades the aqueduct calmly declares that by its completion, almost two thousand years ago now, its builders had accomplished, once and for all, a tremendous task. Hewn stone lies on hewn stone or thrusts diagonally downward against hewn stone, each held immovably in place by its own dead weight. The railroad bridge, by contrast, is entirely preoccupied with what it is doing. Its trusses and girders are a web of members in tension and members in compression, arranged in supple, asymmetrical equilibrium. The stones of the aqueduct rest there,

The photograph of the Pont du Gard, near Nîmes, France, is reproduced from Charles S. Whitney, *Bridges, A Study in Their Art, Science and Evolution,* New York, William Edwin Rudge, 1929. The photograph of the Canyon Diablo Bridge in Arizona, on what was then the Atlantic and Pacific Railroad, is reproduced from an original in the historical files of the Santa Fe Railway. The ironwork was fabricated by the Central Bridge Works in Buffalo, New York, and shipped to the site for assembly.

block on block, sustaining the trough through which water once flowed. But the bridge's trusses gather up and direct the forces set in motion by the trains which the structure quite literally "carries" across the canyon.

Anyone who looks at the Canyon Diablo bridge with eyes accustomed to the forms and proportions of traditional Western European construction will feel a disparity between the apparent fragility of its members and its demonstrable capacity to bear weight. An architecture based on the scheme of forms the bridge embodies would disappoint all the expectations which Western architecture has ratified for centuries. For the disposition of mass, in architecture, has traditionally conformed to what Geoffrey Scott called our sense of "powerfully adjusted weight."* Architecture, indeed, has selected for emphasis those suggestions of pressure and resistance which, as Scott says, clearly answer to our "habitual body experience" of weight, pressure, and resistance.

Since a scheme of forms based upon the tensile strength of steel does not answer to this internal sense of physical security and strength, we cannot enjoy it, Scott insists, even if we can understand intellectually why the structure does not collapse as our eyes convince us it should. "We have no knowledge in ourselves," he says, "of any such paradoxical relations. Our aesthetic reactions are limited by our power to recreate in ourselves, imaginatively, the

* My quotations from Scott are to be found in his eloquent study of *The Architecture of Humanism.*

physical conditions suggested by the form we see."

This so-called "humanistic" conception, of architecture as an art which projects into concrete, three-dimensional form the image of our bodily sensations, movements, and moods, would necessarily exclude all structures based upon the system of tension embodied in the Canyon Diablo bridge. But many structures embodying a scheme of forms in tension do, in fact, give genuine aesthetic delight—including, most notably perhaps, the great suspension bridges of our time. One suspects that Scott's elaborate thesis is in essence only a subtly conceived justification of a long-established "custom in the eye."

The science of the modern engineer, which evolved the unprecedented structural webs of tension and compression, is like nature in that it requires from objects only such security and strength as are in fact necessary. One has only to think of the spider's web or the sunflower's stalk to realize the truth of Scott's observation that the world of nature is full of objects which are strong in ways other than those which we are habitually conscious of in our own bodies. But although there is an order in nature which the scientist can comprehend, it is not, according to Scott, an order which can be grasped by the naked eye. It is not "humanized."

There is an implication here that the eye of science—what we can "see" with the aid of photomicrographs, X rays, stroboscopic cameras, microscopes, and so on—is not "human" vision, and that human life, and the arts which express its significance, are alike alien not only to science but to nature itself. It may be so, but there is much in the vernacular which argues the contrary, and much to suggest that the technological forms which are a part of that vernacular can beget a new "custom of the eye." We would do well, therefore, to set against this concept one which was expressed by a Tennessee architect named Harrison Gill.*

What distinguishes all truly modern architecture from all architecture of the past is, Gill argues, the very fact that it does not rely on compression alone, but employs tension as well. By its use of tension it "comes closer to the forces and mechanics of nature than ever before . . . The ability of a stalk of corn to stand erect lies in the tensile strength of its outer layers. Man and beast can move and work because of the elastic tension of tendon and sinew. All living things exist in a state of constant tension. . . . All truly modern building is alive."

Here, then, from vernacular roots a scheme of forms has evolved which is capable of expressing a humanism which takes man's mind as well as his body, his knowledge as well as his feelings, as its standard of reference, a humanism which sees man not as a stranger trying to assert his permanence in the midst of nature's inhuman and incomprehensible flux, but as a sentient part of nature's universal process.

* In his article, "What Makes Architecture Modern?", *Harper's Magazine,* July 1953.

Up Tails All*

THE THEORY
OF THE DETROIT BUSTLE

* This essay is a revision of a paper delivered as the keynote address at the International Design Conference in Aspen, Colorado, June 23, 1957, subsequently published without the author's knowledge or consent in *Arts and Architecture*, March 1958.

WORDS ARE A POOR MEDIUM in which to communicate ideas about design. Discussions of design, by laymen or professionals, have to be carried on in terms of verbal symbols, but verbal symbols are almost absolutely incapable of communicating any precise or exact conception about tactile or visual experience. If any of us tried, with words alone, to describe precisely the difference between the 1957 and 1960 Cadillac, we would find ourselves hopelessly enmeshed in a clutter of words, which no one else would have the patience to listen to and from which no one who was not already visually acquainted with the two cars could possibly get anything but the most blurred and inaccurate sense of what the two cars look like.

Anyone who reads what designers and critics of design have said at various times in the past soon becomes aware that words such as *function, structure, simplicity,* and *elegance* are so imprecise as to be meaningless. A book published in 1877 about the *Industrial Art* which had been exhibited at the Centennial Exhibition in Philadelphia the year before, reads as if it might have been written by a fairly advanced (if somewhat coy) twentieth-century critic, with its condemnation of showy and flashy objects, "overloaded with meaningless ornament," and its praise of "true honesty in construction, fitness of ornament to material, and decorative subordination." But when one looks at the illustrations of the objects which are praised in these terms, it is perfectly clear that the words "honesty in construction" and "fitness of ornament to material" were verbal symbols of an actuality which does not resemble what we would symbolize by those words. I think especially of a huge piece of furniture, a vast mirror frame with pedestal, carved out of wood by an Italian craftsman in imitation of ruined stonework, with broken columns, a crumbling entablature, chipped statues, and a bas-relief frieze, all overgrown with carved wooden vines in which carved birds disport themselves. The devout carver has even contrived to represent places on the massive base of his creation, where thin slabs of plaster have flaked off of what had pretended to be solid blocks of (presumably) marble, revealing the (carved) brick and mortar on which the (carved) fake masonry had really been constructed. In other words, a man who seriously admired what he verbally symbolized as "honesty in construction" and "fitness of ornament to material" could—in 1877 at least—praise an object which was a wooden imitation of a plaster and brick imitation of masonry.

Carved Wood Mirror Frame, exhibited in the Italian Court of the
Centennial International Exhibition at Philadelphia, 1876 (wood
engraving reproduced from Walter Smith, *Industrial Art*—Volume
II of *The Masterpieces of the Centennial International Exhibition*,
Philadelphia, Gebbie & Barrie, [1877]).

It would be easy to multiply such examples of the imprecision of the verbal symbols we apply to visual experiences. But, besides being visually and tactilely imprecise, words as symbols are peculiarly subject to changing contexts. The whole group of word symbols clustering about the concept of the machine—a concept of great importance to contemporary design—provides striking evidence of this. As an illustration, take the famous passage in which Samuel Taylor Coleridge defined organic form. In a lecture on Shakespeare, given in 1818, he made a distinction between what he called mechanic form and organic form. Form is mechanic, he said, "when on any given material we impress a predetermined form, not necessarily arising out of the properties of the material." Organic form, on the other hand, is innate; shaping itself from within, as it develops, so that "the fulness of its development is one and the same with the perfection of its outward form."

We are all so used to this formulation, or to echoes of it in hundreds of later writers, that we are not likely to wonder why Coleridge used the word "mechanic" as the verbal symbol for the antithesis to "organic." Actually, the adjective "mechanic" like the noun "machine" had strongly disagreeable overtones in 1818. For one thing, it still carried its eighteenth-century meaning, defined in Dr. Johnson's great *Dictionary* as first, "mean, servile, of mean occupation," and only secondarily as "constructed by the laws of mechanicks." Similarly, Dr. Johnson defined a mechanic (i.e., one who works according to the laws of mechanics) as "a manufacturer; a low workman." By 1818, however, the word had taken on still more disagreeable overtones, thanks to the horrors accompanying the industrial revolution. Only five years before, in 1813, the leaders of the violent Luddite anti-machine riots had stood trial in York-shire, and only a few months earlier, Mary Shelley had mesmerized the reading public with Franken-stein's monster—the symbol of the machine as master and destroyer of its creator. To Coleridge and his contemporaries, therefore, and to many since his time, the verbal symbol "mechanic" seemed appro-priate as a contrast with "organic" because it had connotations not only of meanness and servility, but also of inhuman power, of anti-life.

The All but Celestial Mechanics

We need not trace here the subsequent rami-fications of this idea. We are all aware of the preva-lence of the notion that the machine is the enemy of life, and of man. All I need point out is that in the field of design, the effects of Coleridge's verbal symbol are unfortunate. There is no reason why machine-made products should be any less organic in form than those made by hand. Nothing could be more "mechanic," in Coleridge's sense, than the hand-carved Italian mirror frame I just described; both the carved frame itself and the pseudo-masonry architecture it counterfeited are horrendous examples of predetermined form imposed upon material without regard to the material's properties. Yet there has been an anti-mechanical bias in much discussion of design ever since Coleridge's time. People of education and refinement, the vast majority of those who have run our museums and taught in our schools and colleges—the custodians, in short, of the cultivated tradition in our society—have retained the anti-machine bias inherent in the verbal symbols which Coleridge quite understandably used in 1818, but instead of which, at a different moment in history or in another social context, he might well have chosen some other word, such as "arbitrary" or "dead."

In opposition to the cultivated tradition, however, there has been, in the United States especially, for well over a century, a vernacular tradition in which the machine has been unself-consciously and enthusiastically accepted. In this tradition, the word "mechanic" has had connotations very different from those it had for Dr. Johnson and Coleridge. As early as 1843, Horatio Greenough, in one of the essays which provided the first full statement of an organic democratic aesthetic as applied to design, pointed out that it was America's mechanics, not its artists (of whom he, by the way, was one), who had discovered, in designing ships, machines, scaffolding, and bridges, the basic principle of organic design, a principle which (anticipating Louis Sullivan) he phrased as "the unflinching adaptation of form to function." And twelve years later, in 1855, one of the most extraordinary and most neglected men in our intellectual history, Thomas Ewbank, published an astonishing volume entitled *The World a Workshop; or, the Physical Relationship of Man to Earth,* in which mechanism is envisioned as the type of God's creation—not just in the eighteenth-century sense of Celestial Mechanics, but in the sense that everything in and on the earth and in the heavens is made up of the same elements which carpenters, smiths, and other artificers work in, and that it is man's first and last duty to work with matter according to the laws of mechanics, thus imitating his Creator. Men speak of "the Architecture of the Heavens" and of God as the Great Architect, because, Ewbank says, these terms are "more in unison with current ideas of respectability" than terms like mechanics and mechanician. But they do so wrongly, because "with the works of architects we necessarily associate ideas of fixedness and immobility, while motion and change of place are essential characteristics of the universe. It is a display of forces and motions—there is nothing at rest." To control these forces, to manipulate matter, was man's reason for being, and of all men it was the mechanics, he maintained, who worked most intimately with the very stuff in which God revealed his nature and purpose.

No doubt few of those who designed or worked

with machines in nineteenth-century America, or elsewhere, consciously held such exalted notions of mechanics as did Ewbank, even though his work as U. S. Commissioner of Patents and as an active member of the Franklin Institute, together with his voluminous writings, gave him much broader influence than our historians have realized. But, whatever their notions may have been, men like Eli Whitney, Oliver Evans, Elisha King Root, George Corliss, and William Sellers evolved mechanical forms which were as "organic" in the Coleridgeian sense as any ever designed in the tradition of handcraft.

The history of design in America, as I have tried to show elsewhere,* is essentially the product of dynamic tensions between the cultivated and vernacular traditions. Ironically, the cultivated tradition, whose patrons have by and large been uninterested in, or downright contemptuous of, the machine, has been chiefly responsible for inspiring and patronizing those forms which Coleridge labeled "mechanic," while the vernacular, evolved by men who were often mechanics working with machines, has produced those contemporary forms which are most truly organic.

This is not to say that all machine-made objects are organic, or that all handmade objects are mechanic; the interaction of the cultivated and ver-

* *Made in America,* Doubleday & Co., Garden City, 1948. Re-issued in 1957 by Charles T. Branford Co., Newton Centre, Mass.

nacular traditions is more subtle and complicated than that. It is only to say that the worst machine-made objects are those whose designers have been most awed by the prestige of the cultivated tradition, just as some of the worst handmade objects have been those whose designers made foolish concessions to a hot-house-cultivated "aesthetic of the machine."

The fact that cultivated forms have influenced vernacular forms is familiar to all who have seen nineteenth-century locomotives with Gothic or Palladian windows in the cabs, and stationary steam engines whose framing is done with Doric or Corinthian columns. Less often noticed are the examples of the reverse influence of vernacular forms upon objects designed in the cultivated tradition. It is especially easy to overlook these because, in recent years, the vocabulary of designers and critics has been optimistically overeager to blur distinctions between the two traditions.

For an instructive example of the vernacular's influence on the cultivated tradition, we might look again at the spring-steel cantilever chair which Mies van der Rohe designed in 1927. The two basic elements in this design were the cantilever principle (which Mart Stam, of Holland, had used in a chair he designed the previous year) and the spring principle of bent steel. Both of these principles had been used in seats long before, but only in those vernacular areas where "artistic" effect was not consciously attended to. As Mart Stam himself said, he found the suggestion for his original cantilever chair in the folding jump seats used in seven-passenger American automobiles. As for the spring-steel principle, it had been used for eighty years or more on the cantilevered seats of American agricultural machines (combined, incidentally, with a seat which was functionally shaped to fit the human fundament in its pear-shaped, seated position).

All this has been noted before. But what I, at least, overlooked till now is that both of the vernacular designs were functional, while the Mies van der Rohe design—so widely hailed as a masterpiece of functionalism—was not. Both the jump seat and the mower seat were functional cantilevers, because back legs on the jump seat would have interfered with the feet of the passengers sitting behind them, and there was no part of the mower to support back legs for its seat, which was cantilevered out over empty space so that the operator could sit behind the cutter bar and see what it was cutting. As for the spring effect in the mower seat, it provided a functional shock absorber on a rough-riding machine. For household chairs, however, which are used on relatively flat surfaces which don't jounce, neither the cantilever nor the spring was quite relevant. The Mies van der Rohe design was, fundamentally, pure playfulness—the product of cultivated aesthetic playing solemnly with forms developed in the vernacular.

Off Again, on Again, Fins Again

In recent years, since about 1930, the prestige of genuine vernacular forms has enormously increased, partly as a result of social and economic forces which, during the depression, made economy and simplicity attractive, and partly because in those years certain vernacular forms (especially those of the airplane) reached a degree of refinement which gave them an unimpeachable appropriateness and made them a source of liberated delight. Aerodynamic forms have, in fact, acquired an authority as classically absolute as the sculptural forms of Periclean Athens, the blank verse dramatic forms of Elizabethan England, or the choral forms of eighteenth-century Germany. And, as Dr. Jacob Bronowski said, in a speech published in *Industrial Design,* because these vernacular designs (he calls them pioneer designs) interest and satisfy us, "there grows from them a custom in the eye" which forms our taste in other fields as well. We like to design and to buy streamlined toasters and irons not (as Dr. Bronowski sensibly points out) because we have any expectation of their flying, but because machines that fly have taught us to question protuberant decoration and to admire streamlined forms. To me it seems likely that it is to this magnetic appeal, rather than to the Freudian symbolism in which some critics are so artlessly absorbed, that we owe

the rocket-shaped ornaments and tail fins of contemporary Detroit.

I am convinced that if we could really determine why the designers designed those tail fins, and
why the car-buying public liked them, we could
clear up some of the confusions which befuddle
many of our opinions and judgments about contemporary design. In this connection, I am reminded of
an idea I encountered in Don Wallance's book,
Shaping America's Products, which may serve as a
useful text for further discussion. Mr. Wallance
distinguishes at one point between objects whose
inner structure and outer form are integral—such as
a pottery bowl or a plywood chair—and, on the
other hand, objects whose outer forms merely
sheath an inner structure or mechanism—objects
such as refrigerators or radios, whose essential nature
separates the process of making from the process of
designing. Like all verbal classifications, these are
useful only so long as we stay in the middle of
them, keeping clear of the peripheries where the
distinctions become blurred. But, if we do stay in
the middle, we can, I think, get a helpful perspective
on those much-maligned fins and on other contro-
versial aspects of design.

When we consider objects whose inner structure and outer form are integral—such as a tea cup
or a glass tumbler—it seems to me that we can all,
designers and consumers alike, agree upon what
constitutes good design. We can without too much

difficulty determine whether the design is appropriate to the tools with which it is made, to the materials of which it is made, and to the uses for which it is made; whether it has evolved from the inner structure; in short, whether it is organic and functional.

In considering objects of the other class, whose outer forms merely sheath an inner structure which designer and public agree should be covered up—such as an eighteenth-century grandfather clock, or a twentieth-century toaster—we are, however, in an area where the question of the appropriateness of the design becomes much more complicated, becomes, in fact, not a matter of logic, but of taste. And we may as well define taste, right now, as that sort of preference for one or another form which is relevant only when form is independent of function. Or, to put it differently, taste is that sort of form-preference which can logically be illogical, and usually is. Taste can have little to do with the design of an airplane wing or a propeller blade, but almost everything to do with the design of a refrigerator cabinet or a woman's dress.

It was, I think, to the failure to distinguish between these two classes of objects that Raymond Loewy was objecting when he said some years ago that he couldn't go along with those critics who brand the shell or wrapper treatment as a breach of design integrity. If so, I heartily agree with him. But, in making his counter-argument, Mr. Loewy seems to me to have reinforced the confusion instead of clearing it up. An airplane, he pointed out, is internally a complex arrangement (I think he said messy) of gadgets, wiring, tubes, dials, ducts, spars, levers, rivets, and controls. Everything is functionally correct, but it would look extremely confusing if it showed. It is only the airplane's skin, or shell, Mr. Loewy maintains, which by covering this internal confusion makes the airplane a form of such elegance. And from this he concludes that "when a given product has been reduced to its functional best and still looks disorganized and ugly, a plain, simple shield . . . is aesthetically justified." This shield, he argues, becomes functional, "the specific function being to eliminate confusion."*

Now, much as I admire Mr. Loewy's plain and simply shielded locomotives and several other designs of his, I think it is worth pointing out that he is cheating in this passage; because the skin of an airplane is not a simple shield at all; it *is* the airplane; it *is* the organic structural form of the object, into which all those gadgets, tubes, dials, and ducts must be stuffed as neatly as may be. It is not, like a refrigerator shell or a clock case, something which can be one shape or another, fussy or plain, angular or rounded, according to the designer's or the consumer's whim. Mr. Loewy happens to have (or at least had when he wrote his book) a taste for nonangular simplicity. Elsewhere in the book he lays

* *Never Leave Well Enough Alone,* Simon & Schuster, New York, 1951.

it down as a law of design that "the general mass [of an object] should be flowing, graceful, free of sharp corners and brutal radii"—which, of course, is not a law of design at all, but merely a manifesto of taste, and one to which some very eminent designers, including the designer of the Pyramids, and Charles Locke Eastlake, and Mies van der Rohe, to name some diverse examples, would not have subscribed.

I happen to prefer Mr. Loewy's designs to those of Charles L. Eastlake. All I am trying to point out is that there is a difference between the skin of an airplane and the shield or sheath which covers an automobile engine or a toaster mechanism, and that it is useful to avoid confusing the two. To justify the hood of an automobile engine by analogy with the nacelle of a plane tells us something about the contemporary prestige of aerodynamic form, but nothing at all about what good design of an automobile is.

Think again of the Cadillac's famous (or infamous) fins, or of their exuberant progeny on other cars. In Don Wallance's terms, these forms are sheaths, in no sense integral with the inner structure or mechanism of the car; and as I have suggested, there is no reason why they shouldn't be sheaths, or why we should try to apply to them, or to any other sheath design, the criteria we apply to integral designs. They are not functional, in Greenough's sense, nor organic in Coleridge's, and it strikes me as silly for the advertisements to try to pretend they are. I am convinced those fins are the shape they are primarily because some designer liked their looks, and because a good many car buyers (*not* including me) agree with him. I am also convinced that both the designer and the buyer like the look because the fins echo forms which were functionally evolved in aerodynamics and are therefore pleasing.

If we are going to use the term functional in our discussion of design, let us agree that it has two quite different meanings, one of which applies to integral design, and one of which applies to sheath design. One kind of functionalism has to do with the appropriateness of design to tools, material, and use, and tends toward simplification and what Greenough calls "the majesty of the essential." The other

The prototypical "tail fins." Detail of the 1948 Cadillac (photograph courtesy of General Motors Photographic Section).

kind of functionalism has to do less with the structure of the object than with the structure of the designer's and the consumers' psyches, and tends whimsically toward the simple or the baroque, depending on lots of things which we needn't here be concerned about. To keep it separate from the other sort of functionalism, why don't we simply and honestly label it effective packaging?

Most features of automobile design, or "styling," as it is more significantly called, like most features of toaster design and dress design, are packaging in precisely the sense that the wrapper for a bar of candy and the box for cereal are packaging. The couturier's bustle and the Detroit car stylist's bustle are to be judged by the same standards, and effective packaging does have its own standards (some of which, of course, are utilitarian) which merit serious and respectful attention in their own right, undiluted by carry-overs from integral design. It seems to me that the sooner we all—designers and public alike—stop confusing the two, the sooner we will be able to agree upon what we are talking about in our discussions of design.

Those tail fins are as "functional" as the shape of a bomber's wing, though their function is less utilitarian. They have, of course, some utilitarian functions. They do hold the taillights up high, where they are more visible than taillights used to be in traffic, and they are said to serve some aerodynamic function at high speeds. But their chief function was to delight the eye and attract buyers, which is the principal function of all packaging in our economy. This they did, superlatively well. The fact that some of us had other ideas about what a suitable package for the rear end of a car should be proved only how wrong we were.

We were wrong, I think, because we persisted in thinking of automobiles as pure vernacular designs. Most of us who disparaged the tail fins were admirers of the army jeep and its early civilian counterpart, whose design frankly acknowledged that it was a four-wheeled vehicle with a motor up front. In this respect the jeep was a direct descendant of the Model-T Ford, solidly based in the vernacular: a mechanical form which was almost wholly "organic" in Coleridge's sense.

The finned Cadillac, on the other hand, was a sheath design. Coleridge would have called it "mechanic," in the sense that the fins and other elements of the design were "predetermined" forms imposed upon the material. But as I have tried to show, this does not mean that the Cadillac sheath was non-functional. It means only that the function it served was non-utilitarian, having more to do with the psychological uses of an automobile than with mechanical transportation.

What we must not overlook, if we are interested in American developments in design, is that the predetermined "mechanic" forms employed in this tremendously successful and influential sheath design were not borrowed from the pre-industrial handcraft tradition. They were borrowed from another area of design rooted in the vernacular: from the airplane, which even more than the automobile, epitomizes the concern with motion and mobility in our technological civilization. Like almost everything designed in our culture, those finned Cadillacs are a product of the dynamic tensions between vernacular and cultivated influences. But it is a mark of how far we have come since the Centennial's ornate pedestaled mirror frame that the "cultivated" forms here applied to an object which emerged from the vernacular are forms which had themselves been developed and refined from other vernacular sources. Our vernacular, in some areas at least, has become a cultivated tradition of our own.

Soft Sell, Hard Sell, Padded Sell*

* This essay, in slightly different form, was written to be read at the University of Michigan,
May 13, 1960, as one of a series of University
Lectures, by various speakers, on Advertising
in American Society.

A FEW WEEKS AGO I saw a television commercial which showed a man—an "ordinary Joe," a you-and-me sort of fellow, with loosened tie and un-buttoned collar—looking at television commerciais. A voice in the background, accounting for the man's changing expressions of dismay, explained that the man was watching a series of commercials for various brands of cigarettes, each of which promised him some special delight. We were not shown the various commercials he was watching; we saw only his face and body as he reacted to them. Finally he saw a new commercial, advertising a new brand of ciga-rette which combined all the virtues of the other brands. His face relaxed; he smiled contentedly and sank back in his overstuffed chair; and the an-nouncer's voice said, "Lucky Joe! He doesn't have to watch the commercials any more."

The implications of this filmed advertisement seemed to me to be interesting. What is going on in the advertising business when an advertisement im-plies that one merit of the product is that, having discovered it, you don't have to look at advertisements any more? My interest was further aroused when I discovered, some days later, that this particular commercial had won a top award in the industry's own annual competition sponsored by the Art Directors' Club. Are we faced with the possibility that the advertising men are getting self-conscious about how boring some of their advertisements are? Is it possible that the trade is even more bored by a good deal of what it is doing than the audience is?

If this particular TV commercial were an isolated phenomenon, it might not be important. But it strikes me that there are a number of recent ads which reflect an amused disenchantment with the tenor of advertising in general. I think, for instance, of Bert and Harry Piel and their irreverent mockery of stale advertising techniques; of a Kaiser Foil ad, cast in the form of a burlesque soap opera; and of a job-wanted ad which ran in the New York *Times* recently, in which a young woman, looking for a job as a copy writer in an advertising agency, began her appeal with: "Soft sell, hard sell, padded sell. From Paris frocks to cuckoo clocks . . . you name it. I've done it, proud!" And one has only to read the editorials, and the letters from readers, in such a trade publication as *Advertising Age* to be aware of how much earnest and responsible self-criticism the advertising men engage in.

In looking at advertising as an aspect of American culture, I am functioning as a non-expert. My knowledge of the business is limited to the impact its products have upon me and my friends and acquaintances, and to what I have picked up unsystematically from a few friends who are in various branches of the business and from desultory reading about it. I have not read any of the best-selling books which, I gather, have exposed the inner workings of Madison Avenue, and I have only glanced at such scholarly studies as Neil Borden's *Advertising in Our Economy.* My approach, then, is that of an interested observer of the American scene, without special inside knowledge of the advertising business.

Like most people I know, I have a nostalgic fondness for the ads I grew up on and the sediment of phrases and pictures which remains from them in my memory: the elegant lines of the 1917 Locomobile touring car on the back cover of *Harper's Magazine;* the Coles Philips "Holeproof Hosiery" girls; W. L. Douglas "pegging shoes at the age of seven"; and such phrases as "not even her best friends would tell her . . ." and "too late for Herpicide." Like most people I know, I am likely to find the advertisements in some contemporary magazines more interesting, visually and verbally, than the editorial matter surrounding them. Like most people I know, I feel insulted by the absurd TV posturing of widemouthed men who hold up cigarette packs or cake mixes and point to the letters on the box as they read them to me, and by the inane posturing of waxen girls with slick smiles caressing refrigerators and washing machines. Like most people I know, I think it is dismaying if people can in effect be forced, by the irrational emotional appeal of advertising, to buy what they do not really want or need; and also, like most people I know, I am sure that neither I nor anyone I know is so naïve as to be unduly affected by such irrational factors. It is just everybody else who falls for the stuff.

It was David Riesman and his collaborators in *The Lonely Crowd* who first suggested, I think, that advertising may be essentially "a fantastic fraud, presenting an image of America taken seriously by no one, least of all by the advertising men who create it." By ripping the suggestion out of the context of Riesman's argument as a whole, I deprive it of its subtlety; but the skeptical attitude it suggests is perhaps a healthy one in which to begin our consideration of a subject about which many of us have firm but conflicting opinions. There are, at any rate, some startling data which suggest that advertising is not quite doing the job it pretends to be doing (and which its impassioned critics too readily give it credit for). A recent survey by Trendex, the TV rating service, indicated that less than twenty per cent of those who watch the popular "Peter Gunn" show know what products the show is sponsored by and that a quarter of those who watch "Alcoa Presents" don't know who sponsors it.

The field of advertising is so broad, there are so many kinds of advertisements, with so little in common, that we should limit our discussion in some way. When I think about advertising, I think chiefly in terms of those ads in which picture and text are combined in a layout whose effectiveness depends upon its qualities as a design. But what of the television commercial? What of billboards, and the neon signs which lure us into bars and grills? What of radio commercials, and of the classified ads which constitute such a large proportion of the total advertising in our newspapers? Are the things that may be said of the ads on television equally true of the Classified ads in Sunday's New York *Times?* Which is more significant of our culture: the ads in the current issue of *McCall's,* or the strange mélange in *The Old Farmer's Almanac,* with its glossy insert of double-page color spreads offering *Chiquita Banana's Cookbook,* side by side with crudely illustrated ads with chatty text offering rupture-easers, gladiolus bulbs, and aromatic fish bait, plus a number of ads, mostly in very small type, beginning, "Are you growing too old too fast?" or, "I nearly itched to death for 7½ years," and so on?

Do we lump all these together when we think about advertising as an institution in our society? Or do we merely select, out of the confused welter of different types of advertising, those which our prejudices happen to be excited by? I raise these questions not because I intend to be systematic, but merely as a warning that my generalizations should be tested against a variety of types of advertising, some of which have little in common with the others.

The Ads as Potter's Field

My concern about advertising is a double one. I am concerned about the role the institution plays in our society, and I am concerned about the quality of the advertisements it produces. And since the quality of advertisements must be judged in terms of the function which they serve, let us begin by trying to clarify our notions about what the role of advertising is.

No one who speculates about advertising as an institution can overlook the chapter on advertising in Professor David Potter's book, *People of Plenty*, which grew out of his Walgreen Foundation lectures in 1954. And since one encounters frequent references to this chapter in the comments of professional advertising men as well as elsewhere, references which suggest a widespread acceptance of the analysis it presents, we should consider Professor Potter's argument.

Professor Potter discusses advertising as the characteristic institution of a society based upon an economy of abundance. Advertising, he argues, would never have been a very significant force in an economy of scarcity, because if there is less than

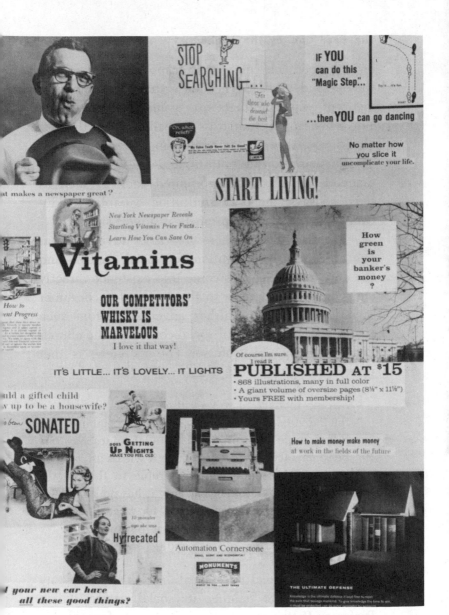

A Confusion of Different Types of Ads (confused by the author).

enough food, clothing, or transportation to satisfy the demand, all that is needed is the mere announcement of what products are available, and where. But when supply outstrips demand, when there is abundance, the role of advertising changes to one of influencing consumer tastes and creating consumer demand. In a consumer-oriented society, such as ours, he says, the only institution capable of educating people to *be* consumers is advertising.

Professor Potter therefore ranks advertising as one of the basic institutions of social control—and the only one which has come into existence directly and wholly in response to the needs of a consumer society. What distinguishes advertising from such traditional institutions of social control as the church and education, in Professor Potter's view, is that there is in its dynamics

> . . . no motivation to seek the improvement of the individual or to impart qualities of social usefulness, unless conformity to material values may be so characterized. And though it wields an immense social influence, comparable to the influence of religion and learning, it has no social goals and no social responsibility for what it does with its influence, so long as it refrains from palpable violations of truth and decency.

It is this social irresponsibility, this lack of any social purpose to balance its social power, which Professor Potter sees as the basic cause for concern about the role of advertising as an institution. He is not unduly troubled by the occasional breaches of taste or deviations from sound ethical conduct which stain the record; one gathers that he would not join those who converted the recent quiz-show and payola scandals into justifications for blanket condemnation of advertising. But neither is he overly impressed by the fairly frequent examples of what he calls "high-minded types of advertising"—the types, one supposes, which are annually applauded by the *Saturday Review*'s awards "for distinguished advertising in the public interest." Neither sort is intrinsic to the institution of advertising as such, he says. What *is* intrinsic, as Potter sees it, is the fact that advertising "regards man as a consumer and defines its own mission as one of stimulating him to consume or to desire to consume."

This might not be bad, one gathers, were it not for the fact that the institution of advertising has a controlling influence in the mass-media: magazines, newspapers, radio, television, and so on. Because of advertising's influence, Professor Potter argues, the mass-media are permeated with efforts to stimulate and exploit "materialistic drives and emulative anxieties" and to validate, sanction, and standardize these drives and anxieties "as accepted criteria of social value."

You may have noticed that Professor Potter is alarmed at the existence of a powerful institution which is not self-conscious about its role as a guardian of social values, which does not seek to "improve" the individual or to "impart qualities of social usefulness." The implication of this alarm, it seems to me, is that the drives and anxieties of the consumer (those drives and anxieties which advertising allegedly stimulates and exploits) are "bad" things and are the result of "wrong" values. Advertising, one gathers, should use its power to change these values and to induce other drives (and, presumably, other anxieties).

For myself, I rather like the idea that modern industrial civilization—this society of abundance in which we live—has produced one institution which, unlike those which survive from earlier and different eras, makes no assumpton that those who control its powerful resources have the duty or the right to impose their values upon the rest of us. Of course I know that individual advertisers do try to use the institution for their own ends, and in support of their particular values. Labor unions sponsor news commentators who are favorable to the union cause and who select and slant the news in their interest, just as a famous machine-tool company runs a full-page ad in national magazines headed "Shouldn't a worker's son have a strike vote, too?" in which it is argued that however a strike comes out, the worker's children will suffer. But the institution of advertising is not committed to imposing a certain set of values and standards upon society; its job is to discover, and appeal to, the changing values and standards which those who live in our society are constantly evolving for themselves. If an advertiser summons up courage enough to assert his own values, he asserts them at his own risk; because, if a considerable number of his prospective customers are offended by his views, they will not respond to his appeal. There are emotional boycotts as well as economic ones.

I do not want to oversimplify here. I am aware that there are techniques, both pictorial and verbal, for creating an irrelevantly favorable aura around ideas as well as products. I know that, from the point of view of sheer logic, there is no reason to travel by jet because an advertisement associates jets with our hopes for the future by showing the disarming rear view of a little boy looking out of what the small type tells you is one of "the DC-8's big picture windows—twice the size of those in other jets." I know that there is no reason to buy a certain brand of sheets because an ad shows them flapping on a clothesline behind a bosomy girl, hanging her largely uncovered attractions over a fence as she tells a male neighbor, "There's not a wrinkle in them, so I think I'll let them wave in the breeze all afternoon." But I also know that there is no reason to buy a particular container because the advertisement associates it with modern art and the great ideas of Western man. Furthermore, I do not imagine that either little boys, or the female breast, or the great ideas of Western man are valued either more or less because of the ads.

There is obviously room for all sorts of conflicting opinions about specific advertisements, specific advertising campaigns, and specific policies in the advertising business. But many of the charges brought against advertising are, it seems to me, charges which should properly be brought against society as a whole. We cannot examine contemporary advertisements as clues to the secret dreams of mass-man, as Herbert Marshall McLuhan has done in his book *The Mechanical Bride,* on the assumption that they are successful because they appeal to certain emotional values which mass-man holds dear, and then turn things about and argue that mass-man holds these values dear because the ads have taught him to do so. The advertising agencies, Mr. McLuhan says, "express for the collective society that which dreams and uncensored behavior do in individuals," but in the next breath he tells us that the agencies, like Hollywood, "are always trying to get inside the public mind in order to impose their collective dreams on that inner stage."

The confusion which underlies McLuhan's analysis—and a good deal of similar criticism of advertising—is related, I think, to a confusion which is evident in Professor Potter's analysis. He classifies advertising as "an institution of social control" comparable to education and the church, and at the same time defines it as an institution which has "no social goals." We can all agree, to be sure, that advertising has considerable influence in our society, but if it has "no social goals" it is hard to see how it can be classed as an institution of social control.

If advertising is, by definition, an institution which came into existence and developed its techniques solely to stimulate people "to consume or to desire to consume," how can we rationally judge its performance by standards which apply only to the work of institutions seeking to improve the individual or "to impart qualities of social usefulness"? We can, of course, lament the fact that an institution of the sort ever came into existence, but this amounts to little more than a wish that the world were not as it is. If we do not like the world which advertising reflects, let us by all means do what we can to change it, but let us not suppose that we can change it by smashing the mirror.

If advertising is the characteristic institution of an economy of abundance, our wish that it more nearly resembled institutions inherited from an economy of scarcity may be wistfully understandable. The wish is unlikely, however, to suggest appropriate standards by which to judge the institution's performance. The products of an institution whose function it is to stimulate consumption should be judged by their success in achieving that end, not by their failure to do other things, however worthy those other things may be in themselves.

The Goods or the Good?

Conflicting views on this subject probably account for much of the contemporary disagreement about what a good advertisement is. For example, none of the medals or certificates of merit awarded in the Art Directors' Club's 1960 competition went to advertisements which received that year's *Saturday Review* awards for distinguished advertising. In the Art Directors' Club's competition advertisements are judged by standards of creative excellence in design. The *Saturday Review* awards committee selects advertisements according to standards of "the public interest"—as that interest is conceived by a board of distinguished educators, editors, publishers, and business executives. The ads which seem best to one group do not seem best to the other, because one group is judging primarily in terms of the message the ads convey and the other is judging primarily in terms of the techniques by which the messages are conveyed.

There is, of course, no necessary incompatibility between creative design and the public interest, though those in charge of the traditional institutions of social control sometimes act as though they thought there were. In architectural design, for instance, the creative developments of the late nineteenth and early twentieth century, which underlie the best work of our own period, emerged in such vernacular areas as amusement parks and industrial plants and were shunned by the churches and universities until, in the normal course of things, they had become themselves traditional and the genuine creators had gone on to other things.

The values of good design, it seems to me, are more appropriate to our judgment of advertisements than those of "the public interest" as defined by educators, business leaders, or public servants. If advertising, as an institution, is by its very nature committed to the view of man as a consumer who is to be encouraged to consume, advertisements surely should be judged on their effectiveness in promoting consumption. If we object, as all of us certainly do, to some of the things the ads try to persuade us to consume (whether those things be stupidly designed cars or attitudes toward labor), we should direct our disapproval toward the sponsor of the advertisement, not toward the copy writers, artists, photographers, and layout men who create the advertisements. To condemn an ad because it skillfully employs verbal and visual techniques to make cigarette smoking seem desirable, when we happen to think cigarette smoking is undesirable, is rather like condemning *Paradise Lost* because we disapprove of its theology and think we know that its cosmology is wrong.

It is interesting, nevertheless, to see how often nowadays irrelevant considerations enter into our judgment of ads, even in advertising circles. The pages of trade magazines in the field are full of evidence that men and women in the business are convinced of the vast power of their techniques for "informing, persuading, and inspiring" and that they want to have clear consciences about their use of that power. A number of advertising executives serve on the *Saturday Review*'s committee of awards. And the Advertising Council, supported by the various advertising agencies, has endorsed and sponsored advertising campaigns in favor of better schools, cancer prevention, support of the United Nations, and other things which its members agree are socially desirable.

All this is no doubt admirable, from the point of view of those who favor better schools, cancer prevention, and the United Nations—as I, for one, do. We may, to be sure, have certain qualms if we remember that a number of thoughtful Americans have reservations about the United Nations; we may wonder whether coming out in favor of better schools serves any very useful purpose unless the emotion is attached to some specific conception of what would make the schools better; and we may wonder whether cancer prevention is better served by pleas to discover it early than by the cigarette filters which advertisements so fervently recommend to us. But in general there is something pleasant enough about having the representatives of such a prosperous institution as advertising devote some of their profits from it to the support of a collateral institution, such as the Advertising Council, whose public gestures are obviously well intentioned.

Furthermore, one can well understand the impulse behind such gestures if one recognizes that the analogy I suggested a moment ago, between an advertisement and Milton's epic poem, is in one important respect inaccurate. The techniques of advertising, unlike the techniques of the poet, are employed to communicate someone else's message, not that of the writers, artists, and designers who create the advertisements. Men and women in advertising are the skilled masters of techniques which are—and must be, in a free society—available to all who want them and can pay for them. In this sense, their business is not unlike that of the telephone company, or of such public carriers as the railroads and airlines. An airline has no more right or obligation to determine whether it is socially desirable to transport me from New York to Michigan or Colorado than an advertising agency has to determine whether it is socially desirable to permit a manufacturer of toilet water to imply that my wife should use his product if she wants to be physically desirable to men who drive Jaguar sports cars.

Advertising, then, is rather like an art in which the techniques have, to a great extent, been divorced from subject matter. The subject matter is provided by the patron, as it were, and the execution alone is the responsibility of the artist. An advertising agency is, to some extent, like a team of poets laureate with not one institutional patron but dozens, each with its own diverse interests to be served, much as if England had a team of poets laureate who had to collaborate on an ode on the merits of nationalized railways, and one on the attractions of British woolens, at the same time that they celebrated the marriage of Princess Margaret. It is a difficult position to be in—especially for people who, like the writers, artists, and designers who produce the advertisements, are by nature and temperament disposed to the lonely responsibility of creativeness. Not that the position of the creative people in advertising is unique; it is not. In the movie studios, and in the corporate journalism of *Time* and *Newsweek*, and in many other areas of contemporary life, similar problems exist. But this team creativeness which the arts grounded in modern technology seem to require presents perplexing problems, not the least of which is the divorcing of techniques from subject matter; and it is no wonder that the people involved have qualms about some of the subject matter to which they have to apply their techniques. Creative people in the visual and verbal arts often have values which are antithetical to those of people who are likely to be successful managers and entrepreneurs in industry—yet it is the leaders of industry who prescribe much of the subject matter on which advertising must employ its techniques. It is no wonder that some of those engaged in advertising, acting in response to the promptings of their individual consciences, either leave the business and write savage novels about it, or work from within, as it were, to make advertising serve some values which seem to them to be "in the public interest."

But I cannot help wondering if such activities are not partly responsible for the aura of pretentiousness which has fallen like a blight on so much contemporary advertising. I may exaggerate, but it seems to me that there is a depressing amount of evidence that advertising is suffering from a sort of stuffy do-goodism, brought on by those who seek to impose upon it values which bear no relation to the dynamics of the institution itself. An institution which arose in response to the needs of a consumer-oriented economy of abundance, based upon modern technology, may have all sorts of faults; but they are not likely to be eliminated or alleviated by attempts to warp the institution into the service of values relevant to other institutions.

Do Public Interest Ads Serve the Public Interest?

Let me illustrate my point concretely. Those who object to the social irresponsibility of advertising, seem to approve heartily the series of advertisements, sponsored by the Container Corporation, which present reproductions of modern paintings in conjunction with quotations from the Bible, or *The Education of Henry Adams,* or some other repository

of what the ads call "Great Ideas of Western Man."
One of the ads in this series won the top award in
the 1960 *Saturday Review* competition.

This series may or may not be effective in increasing the consumption of containers. The late
Walter Paepcke, who initiated the series, said it was
not designed to sell boxes but to establish for his
company a reputation which would in the long run
bring more sales. Admen who approve of the series
point to the fact that company sales have greatly
increased in recent years. Others may wonder
whether increased sales of boxes and containers,
which are sold to other manufacturers as packages
for their products, do not probably owe more to
aggressive salesmen and to the proved quality of the
containers than to the company's "corporate image"
of itself as a patron of the arts and of man's cultural
heritage. But whether or not the ads are good, by
fiscal standards, they seem to be universally ap-
proved in terms of their service to "the public interest."

If we look at the ads in this series from a different point of view, however, and judge them by
standards appropriate to designed layouts of picture
and text, we may discover that the public interest
is less well served by them than we are supposed to
believe. Let us grant that the ads are designed to
induce us to consume the notion that the Container
Corporation of America is a good company because
it believes in the Great Ideas of Western Man (a

later series, by the way, pays homage to the Great Ideas of Eastern Man as well) and also sponsors modern art. And for the sake of the argument let us grant the dubious point that it is because they have effectively induced the consumption of this notion that sales of boxes have increased. And, having made these concessions, let us examine 1960's prize-winning ad.

The "great idea" which the ad celebrates is contained in a sentence quoted in large type from Henry Adams, namely: "A teacher affects eternity; he can never tell where his influence stops." Inserted between the two lines of type which this quotation requires is a color reproduction of a painting entitled "Primeval Wall" which some very small type, running vertically along the right-hand edge of the picture, tells us "represents the ancient cave paintings where the drama of teaching began a hundred million years ago." Except for modest identifications of the source of the quote, and the artist who made the painting, and the sponsoring corporation, neatly placed at the bottom of the page, that is all there is to it.

The ad is obviously intended to appeal to the public's respect for education and for the arts, though it is difficult to see what relevance the representation of the cave painting has to the idea expressed in the quotation. Iconographically, the abstract forms in the picture make no visual communication that in any way suggests teaching, handsome as they are in themselves and in their formal and tonal relationship to one another and to the space defined by the mottled, rectangular background. Nor does the explanatory vertical strip of small type explain very much, with its ambiguous reference to "cave paintings where the drama of teaching began." (Did teaching begin in the paintings or in the caves? Is there any evidence that it began in either place?) There seems to be something pretentious about the juxtaposition of the picture with the Adams text.

And what of the text? Is it in fact a great idea of Western man? Is it not true that a bartender and an operator of a turret lathe also affect eternity and can never tell where their influence stops? Granted that in the context of Adams's book the idea was significant, the isolated sentence can scarcely be called a "great idea." In fact, is there not something pretentious about the whole conception of presenting great ideas in one-sentence capsule form? Is not a great idea one which is, like Willard Gibbs's theories of thermodynamics, or Aristotle's idea about the relations of form and matter, by definition so complex that it cannot be conveyed in a single motto-like sentence?

Even so, it may be argued, the ad implies nice things about teachers, and since teachers are a Good Thing, the ad is surely in the public interest. But of course teachers aren't necessarily a good thing at all; a bad teacher is a very bad thing indeed, especially considering the fact that, like the bartender, he affects eternity. So, much as I selfishly hope, being a teacher, that the prize-winning ad leads to public willingness to provide higher salaries for teachers, I am not really convinced that such a result would be in the public interest unless there were some way to insure that the higher salaries would attract good teachers, not bad ones, to the profession.

What can be said, however, about the prize-winning advertisement's contribution to the worthy cause of modern art? In considering this question we shall encounter, even more directly perhaps than in our discussion of other aspects of the ad, the criteria which seem to me to be relevant to our judgment of advertising.

On the face of it, this ad, like the others in the series, makes part of its appeal by association with contemporary painting. It uses the reproduction of a painting for "eyeappeal," for the attention-getting qualities of design which the reproduction has, and it seeks to identify the sponsoring manufacturer with certain values which the sponsor associates with modern art. As Mr. Paepcke told an interviewer from *Advertising Age* in 1955, modern art was used in the ads because "a packaging firm has to be modern." Packagers, he said, "want sleek, up-to-date material; for that reason we don't think Giotto or Gainsborough would do for us."

One may wonder what service is done to modern painting by exploiting its "sleek, up-to-date" qualities, even though one may acknowledge that

the fees paid to the artists whose paintings are reproduced must be as welcome to them as a raise
in salary is to a teacher. Doing good to modern
artists is not, however, the same as doing good to
modern art, any more than raising my salary is the
same as making me a better teacher.

It is sometimes argued that the cause of modern
painting is well served by making reproductions of
it so widely available, but here we come up against
the technical conditions which are involved in advertising. Magazine advertisements such as those in
the "great ideas" series are reproduced by photo-
mechanical processes. They are printed from plates
made by photoengravers, and the photoengraving
process is such that the colors in a painting are inevitably distorted unless the reproduction is precisely
the same size as the original, and unless its surface has
exactly the same texture. More than thirty years ago,
Gordon Aymar, then art director of the J. Walter
Thompson agency, protested against the use of over-
size oil paintings as the basis for advertisements in
which they have to be reduced to a sixth or an eighth
of their original size. He was, of course, thinking primarily in terms of the added difficulty which the
agency and the photoengravers had in trying to ap-
proximate the color values of the original art work.
To the agency, and the craftsmen in photoengraving,
it made more sense to employ artists to paint pictures
of appropriate size and to work in colors easily
matched by the process-inks which are used in print-

ing plants. But from the artist's point of view, also, the reproduction of a painting in reduced size is undesirable—unless one can conceive of a painting in which color values are inconsequential. In representational painting, perhaps, the iconographic elements of the design may outweigh the color relationships in interest, so that a reduced reproduction, with its inevitable color distortion, may retain the painting's principal values. But in reproductions of modern paintings the changed color values surely distort the essential qualities of the work of art.

Looked at from this point of view, the prize-winning public-interest ad appears to be less favorable to the public interest than it pretends to be. If, as there is some reason to suspect, the ad has also had little effect in stimulating the consumption of containers, either directly or indirectly through creating a favorable image of the sponsoring corporation in the minds of packagers, it is inefficient as well as pretentious.

One turns with relief to the ads which are frankly out to sell a product or a service, by associating it in picture and text with values which potential consumers are likely to admire, and which employ techniques of writing and of picture making which are appropriate to the advertising medium involved —a good photograph of the bottle or the bra. One wonders if, in the end, the public interest will not best be served, in this opulent economy of ours, by freeing the institution of advertising from pressures to adopt values which are alien to it, and by allowing the creative, talented writers, artists, and designers in the agencies to create ads which do the job advertising can effectively do.

It would surely be in the public interest to remember that many, if not most, of our objections to advertising are really objections to some of the businesses and other institutions of social control which employ advertising as a means of competing for our attention. In a free society a wide variety of institutions will forever be engaged in such competition, and in a free society those of us who have one set of values will always be tempted to wish that those with opposing values could be silenced. The constant challenge to our cause, when those with other values have equal access to the skilled techniques of persuading and inspiring, is likely to teach us respect for what Edward Filene called "the intolerable fatigue of persuasion." The danger is that it may even persuade us that, in the interest of our particular "truth," the advertising agency's skilled techniques should be denied to those whose values we disapprove. Freedom is a fatiguing state of affairs. But I like to think, as I leaf through our contemporary magazines, with their wealth of good and not-so-good ads, that freedom is worth the fatigue.

Certainly freedom for the creative people in the advertising agencies is worth it. Most of the advertisements which have won medals in the past few years in the Art Directors' Club's competition were produced by men and women working in small agencies, where individual creative talents are not subordinated—as they tend to be in the large agencies —to market research and the electronic computation of taste. It was one of the small, relatively new agencies which produced that television commercial I began by describing—the one which showed us the lucky Joe who wouldn't have to watch commercials any more. And the delightful thing about that ad for Alpine cigarettes is, of course, that far from making us want to stop looking at commercials, it has just the opposite effect. I will watch any Alpine commercials that come along, if they maintain such standards. I might even switch to Alpine cigarettes.

The Beer Can
by the Highway;*

OR, WHATEVER BECAME

OF EMERSON?

* The earliest version of this essay was written
as an address to be delivered at Mills College,
Oakland, California, April 4, 1957, and was
published in the *Mills Quarterly*. A subsequent
version was published in *Harper's Magazine*,
March 1959, under the title "Waste Not, Have
Not."

Two aspects of American civilization strike almost everyone: the abundance it enjoys, and the waste it permits (if it does not enjoy that too). As a London *Times* reviewer observed, in a discussion of three important books on American history, the occupation and development of this country has been "a wasteful process," and the American god "was not, is not thrifty. Nor is he, or was he, tidy."

Toward this untidy abundance the Europeans' attitude has generally been what George Nelson, the architect-designer, describes as "a blend of appalled curiosity, downright disbelief, righteous indignation, and envy." On what comprehensible basis, they want to know, can a nation "throw away its cars when the ash trays are full" and yet prosper? How, in short, can a nation get richer and richer—achieve more and more abundance—as it grows more and more wasteful?

Of course it is by no means only foreigners who are dismayed. A good many Americans, disturbed by our failure to win friends and influence people abroad, have come to think that we have, in effect, sold our birthright for a very messy pottage, breeding an irresponsible race who litter our vacant lots and our national parks with equal spontaneity. We all feel self-consciously apologetic about this untidiness at times, especially just after we have read the latest best-selling indictment of our culture (usually referred to as "mass culture" nowadays) or just after we have returned from a trip abroad. In such moods we look about at the spasmodic cyclones of gum wrappers on subway platforms, at the sodden banks of garbage between which rivers of industrial waste flow to the sea, at the beer cans strewn along the shoulders of our highways, and we think wistfully of a scrubbed village square in Holland, the poplar-lined embankments of a river in Normandy, or a mathematically clean autobahn in Germany. It would be nice, we think, if America were not so unkempt.

Sometimes we feel the same way about our politics. Back in the 1920's, for example, when we got a glimpse of the political sewage flowing through Harding's Washington, some of us talked enviously of the disciplined efficiency of Mussolini's new regime in Italy. Not that we wanted Fascism, of course, even if the trains did run on time; but the idea of political discipline has its charms when you look at the disorderly machinery of democratic politics.

It is not only our political machinery that is messy; that of our industrial system is frequently messy too. The teams of British technicians, workers, and managers who came here after the war, sponsored by the Anglo-American Productivity Council, were frequently struck by the untidiness of our factories and machines. As one report phrased it: "We found the standard of cleanliness of machines to be lower in America than in Britain. The attitude toward machinery cleaning in America seems to be that it is largely unproductive." But, having noted this, the report went on to say—in words reminiscent of some of Lincoln Steffens's remarks about our political machines—that there was "certainly no evidence that the dirtier machines were working any less efficiently" than the others.

That comment, it seems to me, evokes a paradox which underlies many aspects of our civilization. There are several ways in which the paradox can be stated, but they all add up to something like: "Waste not; have not" or "Nothing succeeds like a mess."

However you state it, it sounds as if it were flippant nonsense; but I suspect it is a clue to our history, nevertheless. And if it is, we had better look seriously at it; for these are times when an understanding of the dynamic of American experience matters a great deal—to our own confidence in ourselves and to others' confidence in us and in the things we profess to stand for.

Who Owns the Joint?

One way to get at the nature of the paradox of waste and abundance is to speculate a bit about the beer can by the highway, which at night picks up the beams from your car's headlights and glows like a panther's eye. Does it mean anything more than that we are a wasteful and untidy people?

Bearing in mind the oft-repeated charge that we are a people who waste a great deal of our wealth and talent upon packages, labels, and surfaces generally, and too little on what is inside; and further remembering that beer cans, like most of our packages for food and drink, are handsome, well made, and attractive; isn't the discarded can, glowing by the roadside, a witness of a countervailing contempt for packaging? Someone who had finished its contents threw it there without a thought, just to be rid of it.

But, it will be objected, the discarded can is also a sign of other kinds of contempt: contempt for natural beauty, and contempt for the rights of others to enjoy that beauty. Perhaps so; but we need not leap too inconsiderately to those conclusions. May it not be simply a sign that the person who tossed it there inhabits a world ungrooved by routine, a world in which he can be so mobile that he need not worry about that can blighting any landscape to which he is likely to return? As for the other fellow's rights: if the man who tossed out the can does not mind other people's discarded beer cans—if, in fact, he rather likes the way they wink at him at night and show him the edge of the road— why should "the other fellow" object to his? Whose highway is it, anyway? And in a world where there is so much natural beauty, whole sierras full of it, whole Alleghenies full, what difference can a few beer cans by the highway make?

Frivolous as such questions may seem, I hope that they suggest that there is a rather tricky relationship between waste (symbolized by those beer cans) and abundance. Everyone enjoys the abundance which enables us to have so many beer cans to throw away, but many of us see no necessary connection between having them and tossing them indiscriminately out of car windows. What I am trying to suggest is that we may not be able to get rid of the mess without also getting rid of the abundance.

From one point of view, the relationship between abundance and waste is a simple one of cause and effect. If we did not have abundance we could not be wasteful. In other words, we are what Denis Brogan calls a people "who go away and leave things" because we have enough and to spare. If we did not, we would take those cans home with us, cut out their ends, slice the remaining tubes lengthwise, and roof our houses with them as the citizens of the depression's Hoovervilles did. If the cause-and-effect relationship is all there is to it, we can make America a tidier and less wasteful place simply by getting rid of our abundance—by giving it away or reducing the efficiency of our productive system.

However, as the roadside beer can suggests, there are other things than a consciousness of abundance which may prompt the American to indulge in litter and waste. One is his mobility, and another is his sense that he is what Pearl Bailey elegantly calls "the character that owns the joint." Now, these are not necessarily the most admirable or endearing characteristics of the American, but they are linked to an element of our environment which is at least as important as abundance: namely, democracy, or at any rate that sort of democracy with which we Americans are familiar. And this raises the question whether waste (and consequent untidiness) may not be as much a result of democracy as of abundance.

There are many who think so; the wastefulness of democracy has frequently been asserted. In a recent book by a distinguished American historian it is flatly said, for example, that after two hundred years of democracy intelligent Americans are beginning to realize that its emphasis on mobility and its denial of status have been excessively wasteful.

A democracy, by definition, must promise people opportunity to improve their standard of living, to develop their individual potentialities, to rise in the social scale, and so on; and that promise has the double effect of putting a premium on all kinds of mobility (social, economic, and geographical) and of requiring the rejection of any fixed system of hierarchical status, whereby individuals are assigned by birth or edict to graded ranks. By this insistence, the argument goes, democracy has bred frightful insecurity and destructive psychological tensions, thereby precipitating what Eric Fromm has called the "escape from freedom" and inducing that flight toward security which has bred the types described in Adorno's *The Authoritarian Personality*.

Dangers of the Closed Frontier

This was all very well, one gathers, as long as there were ample undeveloped resources which people could get by going after them. But now that the real frontiers are closed and we have only what Professor Walter Prescott Webb calls mirages of new frontiers to pursue; now that the unconverted potentialities of abundance have been all but exhausted, it is seriously urged that there is no longer any great need for mobility, and that we must now recapture some of the security that goes with status.

Impressed by such arguments, some Americans are beginning to feel that it is cruelly wasteful, if not socially dangerous, to educate everybody (as the principle of democracy requires us to do) without determining in advance whether there will be jobs available in which they can use their education. Several years ago, at a dinner in honor of General Eisenhower when he was president of Columbia, the then chancellor of the New York State Board of Regents (the head of the state's system of public education) warned against educating more men and women than can earn a living in the field in which they have been educated, lest they "turn upon" the society which aroused expectations that could not be fulfilled. What worried the chancellor especially was that these people would be "better armed in their destructive wrath by the education we have given them." If anyone was reminded of the slaveholders' reluctance to allow the slaves to learn to read and write, no comment was made.

But it is not only democracy's commitment to education which alarms such people. They are troubled too by the way it "encourages people to determine their own goals" and to set their own courses toward them, instead, presumably, of leaving goal-setting and course-plotting to what Ortega y Gasset calls "select and specially qualified minorities." What is the sense of letting people set goals for themselves which the limitations of a disfrontiered civilization will make it impossible for them to reach? The social waste resulting from this sort of thing seems, to some of those who believe themselves "qualified" to judge, too great for our civilization to bear.

From this point of view status now appears to

be something which society must assure, in order to relieve the tensions of insecurity. Hence "togetherness." Hence the widespread approval of the emphasis which the personnel officers of large corporations place upon giving employees a sense of membership in a permanent organization. Hence also the increasing emphasis in labor-union contracts—and in college contracts with the faculty—upon seniority, tenure, and pensions. Hence, furthermore, the popular interest in status variously reflected in such widely read books as Riesman's *The Lonely Crowd* and W. H. Whyte's *The Organization Man.*

From this point of view the beer can by the highway glows with a sinister light indeed, since it is a symbol both of mobility and of a far from reverent attitude toward the decorum of a status-oriented society.

The Goose and the Golden Egg

I do not view the beer can in that light. Those who do so seem to me to misconstrue the relationships between democracy, waste, and abundance. They assume that democracy is a by-product of abundance; that free land and plentiful natural resources are prerequisite to democracy. As for waste, that seems to them to be an undesirable by-product of both the other two. Since they also believe that the available supply of free land and natural resources is on the verge of being exhausted,

225

they regard waste of any kind as something which must be prevented.

I would argue, on the contrary, that a commitment to democracy—and a certain indifference to waste and untidiness—are prerequisite to abundance. I would argue, further, that we and others must learn this quickly because our ability to help create a peaceful world depends upon our ability to maintain our own abundance while helping others to create it for themselves.

By a "commitment to democracy" I mean a commitment to the idea that there are no fixed or determinable limits to the capacities of any individual human being, and that all are entitled, by inalienable right, to equal opportunities to develop their potentialities. Democracy in this sense is an ideal, not a political system, and certainly not an actual state of affairs.

But in order that we may understand one another, let us agree that the term "a democracy" means any set of political, economic, and social institutions, anywhere in the world, which has been shaped primarily under the influence of the ideal of democracy, no matter how much one such set of institutions may differ from others because of local conditions. If, as I think, American institutions have been shaped by the democratic ideal to a greater degree than those of some other nations, that is only because they were established at a time when the democratic ideal was in the ascendancy in the Western world; in a place where there were no already-established institutions which conflicted with or were hostile to democracy; and by people who, having been chiefly "the poor and down-trodden of Western Europe," had little reason to be attached to the non-democratic or anti-democratic institutions still dominant in many areas of European life.

There can be no dispute, I think, about the fact that the two nations which, during the past two centuries, have most successfully converted potential abundance into actual abundance have been the two nations whose political, social, and economic institutions were most fully shaped by democratic ideals: namely, Great Britain and the United States. The only question is whether their success in creating abundance accounts for their having been able to achieve democratic institutions, or whether the attitudes toward man, nature, and God which are embodied in the democratic ideal made it possible for their people to create the unprecedented abundance which they have enjoyed. In other words, which came first, the goose or the golden egg?

The question is important, to us and to all the world, because men everywhere seem to have an insatiable appetite for golden eggs, and one way or another they are determined to get some—by fighting for them if necessary. In so far as we believe that the golden eggs come first, our domestic and

227

foreign policy will consist in efforts to distribute the present stock of eggs equitably enough to keep the hunger for them in check. In so far as we are convinced that the democratic goose comes first, we will do what we can to encourage the growth of any goslings we can discern (whether in Iran, or Indonesia, or Spain, or Russia)—not insisting that they grow up to be geese of exactly the same color and shape and size as ours, and not worrying very much how untidy (or how unimpressed by our status among world powers) they may be.

I am assuming, of course, that the democratic ideal exists, in at least the gosling state, wherever human beings exist, whether or not there are any golden eggs in the neighborhood. It seems a reasonable assumption, since mankind created and cherished the legend of the goose that laid the golden eggs many centuries before the realization of any such dream of abundance was even remotely conceivable. (It is worth noting that, even in the fantasy-world of the legend, the possessor of the goose kills it—as if men couldn't quite allow themselves to attain abundance even in their dreams.)

Certainly the ideal of democracy long antedates the existence of any abundance-creating civilization. Historians are apparently agreed that economic insufficiency characterized all civilizations until quite recent times—say about two centuries ago at the earliest. In all civilized nations up to that time a majority of the people were "inescapably destined to heavy toil and bare subsistence," since the economic surplus was insufficient to provide leisure and abundance for more than a very small minority.

In such circumstances the enviable minority had to keep the ideal of democracy in check if order was to be preserved. To them this would seem neither selfish nor heartless, but plain common sense. Feeling, like all human beings, that the maximum development of human potentialities was an unqualified good, and knowing that it required some leisure and abundance, they naturally wished to retain what advantages they themselves had. They might be (and probably were, at times) sorry for those who did not have it, and might even give some of their surplus away to those whose deprivation was called to their attention. But it must have been clear to them that it was from men and women of their privileged group—not from the lower orders—that one could expect those achievements in the arts, sciences, and professions which most fully revealed the wonderful resources of man's nature. And they must have felt quite justified in trying to avert or stamp out any activity among the vast majority of people which threatened the economic basis of their capacity to enjoy and to exalt humanity's finest potentialities.

To them a system of subordination transmitted by heredity would naturally seem less wasteful and more orderly than one which would—as democratic systems do—conduct what Professor David Potter has called "a great social steeplechase for the purpose of selecting a handful of winners to occupy a few enviable positions." A system of fixed status had the undeniable merit of giving everybody a secure sense that he knew where he belonged and what was expected of him. (It is more than a coincidence, I suspect, that the first issue of *Who's Who*—a reference book which would be of no possible use in a society which knew who who was—appeared in England the year after the revolutionary turmoils of 1848.)

Besides, in a relatively static society with a limited economic surplus, no one had more than a statistically negligible chance for advancement, even if the social steeplechase had been permitted. And even if the hereditary ruling class sometimes had unruly and inconsequential sons, there probably did not seem to be any urgent necessity to recruit new blood from the depressingly underfed, undereducated, and overworked majority. Annoying expressions of hunger for a golden egg could be disposed of by promises of utopia in some distant future, or by such relatively inexpensive distractions as Rome's "bread and circuses" or, later, state lotteries; or at worst by the provision of enough governmental or private charity to silence the most insistent complaints.

The trouble was that, all the while that the very human need to develop one's maximum potentialities was admonishing the privileged few to hold onto what they had, the very same need was constantly fermenting among those who had little. Every now and then some exceptional, or exceptionally lucky, individual rose out of the anonymous mass and got a share of the surplus. Once he had more than the bare necessities, the dynamics of his talent and energy impelled him to disrupt, to a greater or less extent, the relatively fixed status of those at the top.

They, on the other hand, when faced with the energies of a Shakespeare, a Martin Luther, a Napoleon, reacted too late or too sluggishly to preserve unaltered the institutions which such upstarts challenged; with the result that hierarchical institutions in every area of life were forever being modified by pressures from below. For it is axiomatic that security of status, accompanied by abundance, tends to be relaxing. Those who possess it easily succumb to the illusion of permanence. They find it soothing to believe that change, instead of meaning a continuous process of development (and concomitant waste), means only five nickels for a quarter—which is still twenty-five cents. And so, though the process of development and waste goes inexorably on—in human affairs as it does throughout nature—those at the top of the social hierarchy are relatively insulated from the changes which the process inevitably produces.

The upward pressures in Western European civilization had accumulated irresistible force by about 1500. The rapid advances in technology after that time—the swift development of power-driven machines—culminated in the so-called industrial revolution of the late eighteenth and early nineteenth centuries. And that revolution brought abundance within reach of the majority of people for the first time in the history of civilization.

The Brace-and-Bit and All That

It is precisely at this point that we run head on into the question whether the goose or the golden egg came first. Professor Webb's theory of the Great Frontier, as applied to Western civilization in general—like Turner's earlier thesis about the role of the frontier in American history—rests on the assumption that it was the discovery and pre-emption of vast areas of unused land which suddenly made abundance available on an unprecedènted scale, thereby creating conditions favorable to the development of those institutions and qualities of character (including self-reliant individualism) which we associate with democracy. Similarly, Professor Potter has argued (in his influential book, *People of Plenty*) that free land was only one aspect of a total increase of natural resources which—combined with a flourishing technology—produced abundance enough to enable men to afford democracy. Both theories by implication suggest that a sudden increase in wealth was, in effect, the golden egg tossed by fate into the lap of Western man, and that only after men had the golden egg were they able or willing to fatten the democratic goose.

The frontier theory has stimulated some brilliant historical writing, notably Professor Webb's splendid books, and its grand sweep has a tragic persuasiveness. But a skeptical reader is bound to ask why, for example, if the western prairies and plains made the Americans "democratic, prosperous, and numerous," as Turner maintained, they did not have a similar effect upon the Indians, or (as George Wilson Pierson more pertinently asked) upon the Spaniards whose frontier they were before they were ours.

Similarly, if internal social forces in Europe in Luther's time were dynamic enough to cause a religious revolution, one wonders why the stimulus from an external frontier was necessary to incite a technical revolution. Actually—as Lynn White, Jr., and other historians of medieval technology have recently shown—there is a good deal of evidence that the technical revolution was well under way before the Great Frontier of the New World was discovered. The spinning wheel—a key invention of modern technology—dates from about A.D. 1300, and by 1420 an anonymous carpenter or shipwright, probably in Flanders, had invented the brace-and-bit, thereby inventing the compound crank (familiar to you in the form of the crankshaft in your automobile engine) and precipitating what is probably the greatest single revolution in the design of machines. By 1430—sixty years before Columbus—Western man had built machines involving double compound cranks with two connecting rods and was on the way to a Model-T and a Cadillac.

But there are other reasons for doubting that free land is the cause of either democracy or abundance. It was Spain, not England, which first had direct access to the New World's wealth in its most easily convertible form—gold and silver; but it was England which became the breeding ground of democratic institutions. In our own country, New England in the nineteenth century was relatively poor in natural resources while the South was relatively rich—but it was New England which developed the technology and productivity to make abundance available while the more "aristocratic" South contributed almost nothing to the development of technology and became one of the poorest regions in the nation.

These and many similar instances suggest, I think, that the golden egg is not immaculately conceived or doled out in a cosmic lottery, but is engendered like other eggs and, like them, must be fertilized. There may be no conclusive proof that democracy was in fact the goose that laid the golden egg of abundance, but the evidence with which I am familiar certainly makes it seem probable.

Who Gets Ahead?

It would be foolish, of course, to underestimate the role of technology in creating abundance. No one need be so naïve as to believe that all you need in order to be rich is to be a good democrat. So, also, it is true that there is a relationship between technology and natural resources. Professor Webb is clearly right in saying that industrial machinery cannot exist "apart from a body of material to be fabricated." But it does not necessarily follow that "it was the great abundance of raw material which put a high premium on improving the tools" of technology, and that it was this high premium, in turn, which fostered the ingenuity, inventiveness, and other traits necessary to produce a system of abundance. If that were so, the ante-bellum South would have outstripped Vermont and Connecticut in developing machines, and the Georgia cracker, not the Yankee, would have been inventive and mechanically adaptable.

It can be much more plausibly argued that people who are inventive, ingenious, and in other respects mobile are more likely than those who relish or depend upon security of status to recognize potential abundance when they see it. They also are more likely to assume that even though no one ever tried to convert a given resource into actual wealth before, it can probably be done. Furthermore, there is a great deal of evidence that a relative paucity of resources, rather than abundance, encourages the improvement of machines and tools. For instance, it was only after wood began to become scarce that we bothered to perfect mechanical saws which didn't produce almost as many pounds of sawdust as of lumber. All the evidence, I think, points to the conclusion that inventiveness, adaptability, and other qualities which tend to foster industrial productivity (and hence abundance) are directly traceable to drives inherent in the democratic ideal, drives which are nourished by political, economic, and social institutions—and I specifically mean to include religious institutions—which are shaped by that ideal.

In this connection it is worth noting that the reports of those Productivity Teams sent over from Britain after the war give no evidence that high productivity shows any correlation with abundance of natural resources or with the security of a system of fixed status. On the contrary, the reports are full of evidence, explicit and implied, that mobility—and the institutions which foster it—are the chief factors in making America's industrial system more productive than that even of Britain, which in turn is far more productive than that of France, let us say, or of Latin America. This evidence is adduced by observers who had no motive for wanting or expecting American institutions to emerge in such a favorable light. Over and over, in these reports, there are remarks to the effect that Americans "accept new machines, new methods, and the use of new materials more readily than their British counterparts"; or that the Americans are more willing than the British "to put opportunity before security."

All this may sound terribly out-of-date and other-worldly at a time when the Russians have made such spectacular advances in the conquest of outer space. If technology is fostered by democratic institutions, how did the Russians get ahead of us? The answer, of course, is that an autocratically directed technology can do almost anything for which it is willing to sacrifice enough. Hitler's Germany proved as much, as did the Kaiser's before it. But the Kaiser's tanks and Hitler's V-1 and V-2 rockets and Khrushchev's sputniks were not abundance, and the productivity of an autocratically directed technology has never yet equaled that of the democracies. Some of us are now so frightened that we think maybe this time it will.

"Belonging" to What?

I do not mean to underestimate the importance of security. I know the psychological damage which may result from excessive insecurity, or from living in an environment which seems at times to frustrate us at every turn. The point I am concerned to make is simply that some of the current assumptions about the relationships between democracy and abundance, mobility and waste, lead to what seem to me to be fundamental misconceptions about what we must do. They lead to fruitless attempts to eliminate insecurity by providing makeshift substitutes for obsolete systems of status, instead of taking advantage of opportunities—inherent in democratic mobility—to minimize the sense of insecurity and to maximize the transmuting possibilities of change.

The aversion to mobility and change, in our time as in the past, springs from fear. They seem to threaten the abundance which now enables us to divert our energies from mere subsistence into channels of creative endeavor and spiritual development. Men individually, and men corporately as nations, are still driven by this inner necessity to realize their human potentialities. They will go to almost any lengths to ward off a threat to those advantages they have already won.

Since an economic surplus is one of the most recently achieved of these advantages, and since even now the vast numbers who lack it remind us of the way in which poverty can warp and dwarf the human spirit, we inevitably set a high value on abundance. The materialism of modern civilization, in this light, seems understandable enough. And if, besides seeming so desirable, abundance seems to us to be something of which there is a fixed and limited supply, it is scarcely surprising that mobility and waste will seem dangerous, while the ideals of status and order (and the hierarchical institutions which reinforce those ideals) will have a renewed appeal.

We must learn that the craving for status is, at bottom, only the human need for a sense of belonging. Historically, this sense of belonging has been associated with a hierarchy of fixed classes, and with the handicrafts and agricultural techniques appropriate to a status-oriented society. We tend, therefore, to overlook the evidence (of which there is a great deal) that one can belong, and have the sense of belonging, to a process as well as to a class. The awareness of process is new, and the institutions of our mobile society—including its religious and educational institutions—are still bedeviled by leftover preconceptions from an earlier order. Consequently, many of us are convinced that the only kind of belonging that matters is belonging to a cozily defined class, be it the "Workers," or the "Upper Bohemians," or the "Eggheads," or some other sociological Sigma Chi whose sweetheart we can be. It is understandable enough, to be sure, but it may well be suicidal.

Fifty Poor Melons

As for the contemporary dread of wastefulness, so eloquently witnessed by the current interest in conservation, it too is frequently linked with the notion of rigidly limited resources. Writing in the *American Scientist* not long ago, Paul B. Sears asked whether human beings can continue to increase not only their numbers but also "their individual needs, their range and speed" without having to come to terms with "the limitations of a finite environment" as other organisms do. Of course his answer, based upon his ecological research and broad experience in the field of conservation, was that they cannot, even in America—because, vast as our resources and space may be, they "still are certainly finite."

Leaving aside the question whether the conquest of space can remove the finite limitations upon resources—and accepting wholeheartedly the ideal of respect for all forms of organic and inorganic nature—I would only point out the danger that, in times of apprehension, a legitimate interest in averting wanton destruction of resources may degenerate into an equally wasteful passion for hoarding them. Conservation may become mere parsimony, and in the name of the love of nature we may become nature's slaves, instead of her partners. We need occasionally to be reminded of the spirit in which the first great American conservationist, George P. Marsh, worked and wrote. If man is destined to inhabit the world much longer, and to continue to advance, he said almost a century ago, he will have to learn not only to put "a wiser estimate on the works of creation" but also to profit materially "from stimulating [nature's] productive energies in provinces of her empire hitherto regarded as forever inaccessible, utterly barren."

We must learn, what nature can surely teach us, that abundance is in a sense a product of waste. As Emerson said many years ago, "nature makes fifty poor melons for one that is good . . . and she scatters nations of naked Indians, and nations of clothed Christians, with two or three good heads among them. Nature works very hard, and only hits the white once in a million throws."

With his reiterated insistence upon "the infinitude of the private man," Emerson is not in high favor in these days of "togetherness" and "the organization man." Yet it might be good for us to look for a moment through his eyes at the abundant and wasteful civilization in which we live.

Looking about him at the American scene near the end of his life, he observed that—in spite of the European economists' doleful allegiance to the idea that the condition of the great body of the people is fated to be, since it always has been, generally poor and miserable—that same "great body" here in America had arrived at "a sloven plenty . . . an unbuttoned comfort, not clean, not thoughtful, far from polished." It was, Emerson knew, an unprecedented condition, and the rules to meet it were not set down "in any history." What we needed, he concluded, were men and women "of original perception and original action, who can open their eyes wider than to a nationality,—namely to considerations of benefit to the human race . . . ; men of elastic, men of moral mind, who can live in the moment and take a step forward."

We need such people more than ever now. And I think that it is from men and women who share Emerson's open-ended conception of man's potentialities—which is the root and seed of democracy—that we will get that open-ended conception of abundance, that refusal to accept limits to potential wealth or virtue or kindness or talent or love, which will enable us to keep all doors open to our own self-fulfillment while helping others to open doors for themselves.

ACKNOWLEDGMENTS

As THE DEDICATION SUGGESTS, this book owes a great deal to Joan Vatsek Kouwenhoven, my wife. If the essays as they are printed here have a clarity they did not possess in their earlier forms, and if they are more consistent with one another in their present juxtaposition than they were, it is primarily because she resolutely pestered me to say, if possible, exactly what I meant instead of merely taking a stab at it and because she has a delightfully meddlesome way of recognizing inconsistencies when she encounters them.

Most of the essays have been published before, often under different titles and usually in considerably different form. The notes at the bottom of each essay's title page indicate its provenance, but do not suggest the degree to which I am generally indebted to the editors of the magazines and the sponsors of the pamphlets in which they were published and to the institutions and individuals who, by asking me to give lectures or addresses, have forced me to grapple with ideas and impressions which would otherwise have floated around helter-skelter. Nor do they indicate my indebtedness, through reading and conversation, to the stimulation of many other minds—both those whose perceptions seemed to me, when I encountered them, to be anticipations of what I was about to say, and those whose views acted as abrasives upon which I could sharpen my own.

Those to whom I am most vividly aware of my indebtedness in these essays include the students who have worked with me at Barnard College and a number of my colleagues on the faculty at Barnard and Columbia, especially my fellow members of the University Seminar on American Civilization. I owe a curiously non-specifiable debt to the Carnegie Corporation, and its president, John W. Gardner, for having allowed me to vegetate for a year as the recipient of the first of their "Reflective Year" Fellowships, during which time some of the ideas in these essays germinated. My intellectual debt to several writers is suggested but inadequately acknowledged by my references in the essays to their work.

In addition I gratefully acknowledge the stimulus and help I have at different times, over the past ten years, received from individuals who have been interested in my work, including: my former wife, Eleanor Hayden Kouwenhoven; Alexander Girard; Thomas Hornsby Ferril; James Marston Fitch; Eric Larrabee; Frederick G. Frost, Jr., and his son Corwin Frost; Lynn White, Jr.; Dean and

Virginia Rusk; John R. Frazier; Walter Prescott
Webb; Russell Lynes; Leo Leonni; Robert E. Alex-
ander; James Real; and my editor at Doubleday,
Samuel S. Vaughan.

Grateful acknowledgment is made for permission to use the following excerpted material: "Fare-
well Architecture" is reprinted from *Architectural
Record*, April 1960, copyright 1960 by F. W. Dodge
Corporation with all rights reserved. "Whatever Became of Architecture?" was published by the Architectural Society of the Rhode Island School of Design
and is reprinted with their permission. "What Is
'American' in Architecture and Design?" is revised
and expanded from an original article in *Art in
America*, Fall 1958. "Liberal Crafts and Illiberal
Arts" is revised from a keynote address given at the
annual Conference of American Craftsmen and published in part in *Industrial Design*, October 1959.

INDEX

Index